a handful of herbs

RYLAND
PETERS
& SMALL

LONDON NEW YORK

Barbara Segall Louise Pickford Rose Hammick

a handful of herbs

gardening, cooking, and decorating

with photography by Caroline Arber and William Lingwood

First published in the USA in 2001
This compact edition published in 2005 by
Ryland Peters & Small
519 Broadway
5th Floor
New York, NY 10012
www.rylandpeters.com
10 9 8 7 6 5 4 3

ISBN-13: 978-1-84172-877-3
ISBN-10: 1-84172-877-2
Text © Barbara Segall, Louise Pickford, and
Ryland Peters & Small 2001, 2005
Design, illustrations, and photographs
© Ryland Peters & Small 2001, 2005
photograph page 41 b © Jonathan Buckley

The Library of Congress has cataloged the
hardcover edition as follows:
Segall, Barbara
  A handful of herbs : inspiring ideas for gardening,
  cooking, and decorating your home with herbs /
Barbara Segall, Louise Pickford, Rose Hammick ; with
photography by Caroline Arber and William Lingwood
    p. cm.
  ISBN 1-84172-028-3
  1. Herbs. 2. Herb gardening. 3. Herbs--Utilization.
4. Cookery (Herbs) I. Pickford, Louise. II Hammick,
Rose. III. Title.
  SB351.H5 S438 2001
  635'.7--dc21
                                    2001031777

Printed and bound in China.

**Essential oils should not be used
undiluted nor taken internally except
on medical advice. No responsibility for
any problem arising from their use is
accepted by the authors or publisher.**

Contents

introduction

Every one of us feels that our own garden is a special paradise, but the herb garden has the edge on them all. There is nothing quite like the rush of sensual pleasure that comes from simply brushing against a lavender bush, or stepping across a thyme or chamomile path.

These attractions don't end in the garden. Herbs can be brought into the house to be used fresh in cooking, or dried, frozen, or otherwise preserved for later use. Some can be transformed into potpourri or used in other ways to perfume and decorate rooms.

In the herb gardens of today, it is not uncommon to find the culinary, medicinal, and folkloric traditions of the past combined with a modern appreciation of attractive plant forms. Most herb gardens are now enjoyed for the power-packed aromatic leaves of herbs such as rosemary, sage, thyme, lovage, and chives, as well as for the simple but enchanting flowers and useful seeds that many herbs offer. It is this continuity of the past in our present homes that makes the bountiful summer harvest of these useful plants so evocative and especially satisfying.

If asked to define a herb, most people would say it is a plant used in cooking, but the true definition is much wider. It includes trees, shrubs, biennials, annuals, and herbaceous perennials that have culinary, aromatic, medicinal, and cosmetic uses. In addition, many are excellent decorative garden plants. Some herbs are used for their foliage and flowers, others for their seeds or roots, and some for all four attributes.

LEFT **Long valued for its healing qualities, echinacea makes a flamboyant display in a bed, with flowers in white, pink, or purple.**

Barbara Segall

super herbs

BASIL
Ocimum basilicum

With an ancient record in folklore and medicinal history, basil is also a highly distinctive culinary herb, especially in Asian, French, and Italian cuisines.

Best used freshly picked, basil can also be frozen in leaf form or in homemade sauces. It combines well with tomatoes for a salad and is the main ingredient of pesto sauce for pasta. It adds piquancy to pizzas and to chicken and lamb dishes.

There are at least 13 different types of basil, varying in foliage, color, shape, texture, and aroma. Flavors range from anise to cinnamon and the sweet, spicy, clovelike scent of sweet basil. Basil can grow up to 18 in (45 cm).

O. basilicum 'Purpurascens' has purple leaves and pinkish flowers. *O. basilicum* 'Citriodorum' is lemon-scented with green leaves and white flowers. Anise-flavored basil has pale pink flowers and a strong taste of anise. The tiny leaves of Greek basil, which grows in the shape of a small bush, offer the fullest flavor.

Plant basil in an herb garden or in containers in late summer, when there is no danger of frost or severely cold weather. In the herb garden, grow it in a sheltered sunny site in light, well-drained soil. If it is grown in a container, basil should be kept well watered in dry conditions.

Basil has traditional uses as a digestive aid and a herbal tonic, as well as being used in aromatherapy.

BAY
Laurus nobilis

Bay leaves were the foliage used
in wreaths to garland winners
and achievers in classical Greece and Rome.

Glossy dark-green bay leaves are part of the bouquet
garni, the traditional herb bundle used to add flavor
to meaty dishes. Bay is also a good flavoring for
sweet dishes, particularly rice pudding and other
milk desserts; its delicate spiciness can be best
enjoyed if the milk is simmered gently with the
bay leaf before the other ingredients are added.

An evergreen tree with shiny, aromatic, spicy
leaves, small yellow flowers, and black berries, bay
can grow to 40 ft (12 m), but is generally slow-
growing, and in containers its height is controlled.
It can be clipped into geometric shapes or grown
as an elegant ornamental standard. Shaped bay
trees in pots are useful in herb gardens as focal
points to mark a meeting of paths or to emphasize
a change of height. 'Aurea' has golden leaves and
makes an attractive color contrast in the herb
garden. 'Angustifolia,' the willowleaf bay, is also
attractive as a container plant and in the garden.

Buy young plants and plant them in spring or fall
in rich, well-drained soil. Although bay will tolerate
light shade, it prefers full sun. Protect young plants
and plants in containers from frost with straw bales,
bubble wrap, or burlap windbreaks. Cut back any
frost-damaged stems in spring. Pick leaves as needed
throughout the year.

Infusions made from bay leaves have been used
to stimulate appetite or to aid digestion.

CHAMOMILE
Chamaemelum nobile

A pineapplelike scent floats in the air when the leaves are crushed underfoot or gently squeezed between the fingers.

This hardy evergreen perennial is distinguished by flowers that resemble daisies, finely cut foliage—and a perfume that takes your breath away. Chamomile is widely used in cosmetics, soothing skin creams, and other medications. Its dried flowers can be steeped in hot water to make a relaxing tisane, but it has no culinary uses. The creeping, non-flowering variety of chamomile tolerates light foot traffic, making it suitable for covering a short length of path or the ground under a bench.

Non-flowering lawn chamomile, 'Treneague,' which has fernlike leaves, is used to create scented lawns and paths. Upright chamomile, which has daisylike blooms, is grown in flowerbeds for its flowers, which can be used fresh or dried. The double-flowered form, 'Flore Pleno,' is an attractive addition to the garden, and its flowers are used to make chamomile tea.

Grow chamomile in light well-drained soil in full sun. It can grow to 8 in (20 cm). Chamomile paths should be kept weed-free or the weeds will overwhelm the chamomile plants, eventually destroying the fragrant pathway.

The flowers, single or double, of upright chamomile have medicinal and cosmetic uses in facial steam baths and hair rinses; they also bring a soothing and relaxing fragrance to a bath. Dried flowers and leaves of chamomile can be added to potpourri.

CHERVIL
Anthriscus cerefolium

Chervil is highly prized in France, where it is often used in omelets and as a component of the traditional *fines herbes* mixture.

A refreshing salad herb, chervil is also useful as a feathery and flavorful garnish. Its light taste combines well with eggs, poultry, and soft cheese. Although best used fresh, the leaves can be preserved by being frozen in ice-cube trays.

Chervil is a hardy annual with pretty fernlike leaves and small delicate white flowers in late summer. It grows to 12 in (30 cm), thriving in a shady site in light well-drained soil. If planted as an inter-row crop, chervil takes advantage of shade from other row-crop plants. It does not like to have its roots disturbed, so sow it direct into the growing site. Water plants well or they will bolt, flowering and setting seed too quickly, and you will lose flavorsome foliage. Pick the leaves through the summer.

Chervil plants can be grown indoors on a shady windowsill, but indoor plants will lack the vigor and flavor of plants grown outdoors. In mild climates, you can also sow seed in late summer for a winter crop, which will need some protection through the winter.

Rich in vitamins, chervil has been used as a treatment for digestive and circulatory disorders.

CHIVES and GARLIC CHIVES
Allium schoenoprasum and A. tuberosum

Chives bring a delicate hint of onion to garnishes and salads.

Chives have spiky green leaves and mauve flowers, while garlic chives, or Chinese chives, have garlic flavor in their strappy leaves and white starry flowers that appear in late summer. The chopped leaves of both types combine well with egg dishes and are useful for garnishes and in salads. Chives are also among the ingredients of the traditional *fines herbes* mixture.

With its attractive flowers and good foliage, chives fit well into the flower garden. They make an informal edging for part of a vegetable garden, and if planted into spaces in paving, will eventually spread to make their own shapely patterns in the paving gaps. The spiky leaves shoot from the underground mini-bulbs in spring. They grow to about 10 in (25 cm), but can be harvested once they are 4 in (10 cm) above ground.

In late spring even spikier shoots carrying the flower buds start to appear. Chive flowers come in a range of pink-mauve tones, as well as in a new form that is green to white. The flower heads, made up of many tiny flowers, are also edible and look attractive in salads. They are at their juicy best just as the buds begin to open.

Chives grow well in containers, but will need extra attention to prevent them from drying out. Young plants can be kept on a windowsill or planted in the sunniest site in the garden.

CILANTRO (CORIANDER)
Coriandrum sativum

Cilantro (coriander) adds piquancy and aroma to curries and other hot dishes.

A short-lived annual, coriander is grown for its seeds and for its deeply cut, parsleylike leaves that bring spice and flavor to desserts and meaty dishes alike. It bears a profusion of tiny white flowers. For the full effect of their flavor to be appreciated, coriander leaves should be added toward the end of the cooking time.

The dainty pinkish-white coriander flowers that appear from early summer are followed by beadlike seeds, which are used in baking cakes and cookies as well as in curries, chutneys, and pickles. The leaves are added to stews and salads or used as a garnish. Plants grow to a height of about 24 in (60 cm). 'Morocco' is a good form for seed production.

Coriander grows well in a sunny spot in light well-drained soil. It needs a long hot summer for best seed production. Sow seeds in spring in the growing site and cover them with a cloche until established. Young plants should be kept well-watered and free of weeds until they are established. Pick young leaves before the mature ferny leaves develop.

Seeds have a tendency to fall before they can be harvested, so the flower heads need to be picked before the seeds are fully ripe. Cover the flower heads and store them in a warm, dry, airy place so the seeds can ripen. Store the seeds in an airtight jar.

DILL
Anethum graveolens

An excellent partner for fish in any form, hot or cold, dill is renowned as an ingredient of the Scandinavian marinated-salmon dish gravadlax.

Its fresh young leaves bring spice to salads, egg dishes, and soups. The seeds, together with the flower heads, are used in pickles, preserves, and chutney. They are tasty with rice and cabbage, or as a flavoring for bread. Ground dill seed is used in curries.

A hardy annual with aromatic feathery leaves and clusters of yellow flowers in midsummer, dill grows to between 2 ft (60 cm) and 5 ft (150 cm), depending on the variety. The seed needs well-drained soil, full sun, and a sheltered site. Sow in the herb garden in spring, once the soil has warmed up. Because dill grows tall, it is not ideal in containers, but containers can be useful for a first sowing.

Water seedlings and thin to 8 in (20 cm). If necessary, support plants with a light framework of twigs. Water regularly in dry seasons, or the plants will bolt and flower, and leaf harvest will be minimal. Pick leaves as needed when they are fresh and young. Harvest seeds for culinary use before they ripen entirely on the plant. Cut the flower heads off the plant, put them in paper bags, and leave them to ripen in a warm dry place. When the seeds are dried, clean off the husks and store the seeds in airtight jars.

Many seed companies differentiate between leaf and seed dill. *A. g.* 'Sari' is a variety grown for high yields of leaves with short stems. *A. g.* 'Herkules' is highly aromatic, while *A. g.* 'Dukat' is selected for its good leaf production. (All these varieties also produce good seeds.)

Dill is used to calm upset stomachs and to alleviate insomnia. Ground seeds are sometimes used as a substitute for salt.

FENNEL
Foeniculum vulgare

Fennel is distinct from bulb fennel, which is grown as a vegetable. Its wispy foliage is one of the delights of the herb garden in spring.

Bright-green leaf shoots unfurl in spring from pale sheaths in which they are tightly packed like small parcels, scented with an unmistakable aroma. The leaves are a flavorful addition to salads and soups. Bronze and green fennel can be combined to make a topping for salads. Both types are good partners for fish dishes. The seeds are also used in cooking and to make teas or tisanes. The flower heads can be used in pickling, and the leaves for flavoring oils and vinegars.

Fennel is a hardy perennial grown for its finely cut aromatic leaves in spring and summer, and umbels of small yellow flowers in summer. It can grow to more than 6½ ft (2 m) and self-seeds—so be ruthless when you see fennel seedlings in spring. The ornamental quality of its foliage makes bronze fennel, *F. v.* 'Purpureum,' rewarding to grow. It has chocolate-brown feathery leaves, which contrast well with the green of ordinary fennel. The aroma is the same.

Grow fennel in a sunny site in rich, well-drained soil. Sow in the growing site in late spring, or in containers in a greenhouse for earlier germination. Either thin or transplant, leaving 20 in (50 cm) between plants. Pick leaves as needed through the spring and summer The seeds should be harvested in the fall when they are ripe. Divide established plants of common fennel in spring or fall.

Traditionally used as a treatment for a wide variety of conditions, fennel is now most closely associated with the prevention of obesity.

GARLIC
Allium sativum

Garlic is the main ingredient of many typical Mediterranean sauces, such as aioli, and is also valued for its health-giving effects. Individual cloves of garlic can be used whole or chopped, crushed, or roasted in their skins to flavor meat dishes, salads, salad dressings, and bread.

Garlic has onion-like foliage and grows up to a height of 12 in (30 cm). It does best if grown in fertile well-drained soil in sun. Planting times vary, but gardeners with cool or cold winters—below 68°F (20°C)—should plant individual cloves in fall, in rows 12 in (30 cm) apart. Keep them well watered, especially in dry periods. Lift bulbs in summer when the foliage has yellowed. Leave the bulbs on racks or in wooden boxes to dry for a day or two in good weather, then hang them up in bunches in a dry, airy shed.

There are several varieties of garlic available, with varying strengths of flavor; bulb and clove sizes also vary. *A. sativum* has white flowers, while *A. scorodoprasum* (also called rocambole) has a mild-flavored bulb as well as edible bulbils mixed with flowers on its flower heads.

Elephant garlic, *A. ampeloprasum*—which has a huge single onionlike bulb—is available at some supermarkets. Buy several bulbs, some to use and some to plant for next year's crop.

Traditionally used in the treatment of many conditions, garlic has been shown to lower blood pressure slightly and to boost immunity; it also has antiseptic qualities.

LAVENDER
Lavandula species

Long valued for its cleansing properties, and associated with fresh-smelling linen, lavender takes its name from the Latin for "to wash."

With gray-green, softly textured, highly aromatic leaves and (depending on species and variety) deep-blue, purple, white, or pink flowers, this evergreen shrub grows up to 40 in (1 m). It thrives in a sunny, open site in well-drained, slightly sandy soil.

L. angustifolia 'Hidcote,' which has a compact shape and produces deep-blue flowers, is a good choice for edging a path or small bed. There are also forms with green, white or red flowers. Some lavenders, including *L. stoechas* and wooly lavender, *L. lanata*, are less hardy and need winter protection.

Lavender is useful as an edging or a hedging plant for a path or small parterre. Provided that you use plants of the same species or variety, the uniformity of shape and color make it useful in formal as well as informal situations. It tolerates clipping into a variety of shapes. Cut back any woody stems in the fall and remove old flower heads left on the plant from the previous season's flowering. Sow fresh seed in late summer or fall. Transplant seedlings to 24 in (60 cm) apart or 12 in (30 cm) if growing as a hedge. Take cuttings in summer.

Lavender has been used therapeutically for its calming effects, as well as in the production of cosmetics and perfumes. Dried flowers and foliage are used to perfume rooms or packed into sachets and hung in closets.

LEMON BALM
Melissa officinalis

Leaves of lemon balm can be used to add a strong citrus flavor to salads.

A powerful lemon scent, released when its leaves are brushed against, and a fresh zesty flavor help tip the balance in favor of lemon balm, which can become invasive in a small garden. It grows in soft mounded shapes that suit the front of a bed.

Lemon balm is a hardy perennial, growing to 40 in (1 m) when in flower. Its rather insignificant flowers are carried on untidy-looking stems from midsummer to fall. Lemon balm can be useful for areas in the shade, as long as it is planted in well-drained but moist soil.

M. officinalis has plain green leaves. *M. o.* 'Aurea' is a golden-and-green variegated form that is very useful for introducing bold splashes of color to the herb garden. *M. o.* 'All Gold' has yellow foliage.

The variegated form of lemon balm in particular combines well with other plants, but its flower stems should be snipped off to encourage leaf production. Once the flowers have formed, the variegation tends to deteriorate.

Cut back flowering stems in the late fall to prevent self-seeding. Pick leaves when required for fresh use and to dry or freeze. Sow seed in spring and divide established plants in fall or spring.

A few leaves of fresh lemon balm in boiled water make a tasty tea, which has traditionally been used to relieve the symptoms of stress and tension.

LOVAGE
Levisticum officinale

Lovage has a strong spicy flavor and a long history in traditional English cooking. Its foliage slightly resembles that of celery.

A hardy perennial with large dark-green leaves, lovage can reach a height of 6½ ft (2 m). Clusters of small pale-ocher flowers, like parsley flowers, appear in late summer. Lovage does best in a sunny site in rich well-drained soil. Water plants regularly until they are established.

Lovage looks attractive near angelica, and if grown at the base of a rose will hide the rose's bare stems. Divide plants in spring or fall every two or three years. Pick leaves when they are needed and seeds when they are ripe.

Lovage adds spiciness to food. Fresh leaves and stalks can be sprinkled into soups and stews for a meaty flavor, or blanched and eaten as a vegetable. Young leaves are delicious in salads and make an elegant garnish for main dishes. Seeds are sometimes added to cookies before baking. They can be crushed and used as an ingredient of mixed-herb marinades, and are valued as a remedy for digestive complaints.

MINT
Mentha species

With aromas and flavors for all occasions, mints also have much to offer in the shape of ornamental leaves and flowers.

Chop mint into vinegar and mix it with sugar and a little warm water to make mint sauce, the natural accompaniment for roast lamb. Mint jelly, made with apples and mint, is also satisfying with lamb dishes. In Middle Eastern countries mint is used in cooked and cold food, as well as in drinks such as mint tea.

The genus *Mentha* includes some 25 species of perennials grown for their leaves, which are usually oval to lance-shaped and toothed at the edges. The ornamental flowers, ranging from deep mauve to light pinkish-lavender in color, attract bees and butterflies.

Mint thrives in full sun in well-drained but moist soil. Set young plants out in spring or fall, and divide clumps that are growing in the ground in the fall. Mint will grow well in light shade and, as long as there is a source of water, provides good ground cover. To restrict its sprawling growth, plant in a deep plastic or tin container, and sink the container into the ground.

Gingermint (*Mentha* x *gracilis* 'Variegata') has a spicy flavor and green leaves splashed with yellow. Pineapple mint (*M. suaveolens* 'Variegata') has wooly-textured green leaves, marked irregularly with creamy white, usually at the margins. Spearmint (*M. spicata*) and peppermint (*M.* x *piperita*)—both vigorous, spreading plants with attractive flowers—have the flavor traditionally associated with mint.

Mint is at its most aromatic before it comes into flower, so cut it back to encourage leaf production. Harvest the leaves through the growing season—they can be used fresh, or dried or frozen for later use.

Mint may succumb to mint rust, which shows as rusty markings on the leaves. Remove the affected plants and burn them, sterilize the soil, and replant with new healthy plants in another part of the yard.

OREGANO or MARJORAM
Origanum species

Oregano and wild marjoram are two names for *Origanum vulgare*, whose spicy aromatic leaves add zest to many meat and tomato dishes, and are an indispensable ingredient in Greek and Italian cuisines.

There are many other species of marjoram belonging to the *Origanum* genus, the more decorative of which can be used as edging plants or in mixed beds. Some marjorams, including sweet marjoram (*O. majorana*), are half-hardy or tender—either grow them as annuals or protect them in winter. They do not require pruning as such; cut back flowering stems in late summer and all stems to ground level in the fall.

Golden marjoram (*O. v.* 'Aureum') and gold-tipped marjoram (*O. v.* 'Gold Tip') provide wonderful splashes of color in an herb garden. Golden marjoram has clusters of pretty tubular flowers in summer. Its foliage is a lemony-golden color and makes a good display in the herb garden—but it should be planted in a semishady site to avoid leaf scorch from the sun. Gold-tipped marjoram has green leaves tipped with gold, and needs to be grown in a site that is not too shady or it will lose the variegation.

Compact marjoram (*O. v.* 'Compactum') grows to 6 in (15 cm), with a spread of 12 in (30 cm), and makes a good ground-covering mat of foliage. Pot marjoram grows up to 18 in (45 cm) and is propagated from cuttings.

Of the several different forms of oregano or marjoram that can be used in cooking, the best are Greek oregano (*O. v.* subsp. *hirtum*) and pot marjoram (*O. onites*). Some, including *O.* 'Kent Beauty' and *O. laevigatum* 'Herrenhausen,' are regarded as decorative plants in the herb garden rather than for culinary use.

PARSLEY
Petroselinum crispum

A basic herb of many cuisines, parsley is one of the main components of bouquet garni. Use the leaves chopped up or whole in salads, as a garnish, or as a flavoring for sauces and soups.

There are several varieties of curly-leaved parsley, with tightly curled mosslike leaves. All grow as low compact plants during their first year and flower in their second year.

Also attractive, but much larger, is flat-leaved parsley—*P. c.* 'Italian,' or Italian or French parsley. It grows to a height of 12 in (30 cm). Its foliage is flat, and the stems and leaves are delicious either in salads or in cooked dishes.

Parsley is a hardy biennial that needs to be handled gently when it is transplanted because root disturbance will trigger its survival mechanism and set it in flowering mode too early. It prefers moisture-rich soil and partial shade. Buy plants in spring or fall. Cover fall-planted parsley with fleece or a cloche in winter to ensure a good supply of fresh herb.

The chopped leaves of parsley freeze well, and whole leaves can be dried for winter use. You can use parsley to make an alternative to Italian pesto sauce (usually made with basil), for parsley butter, and in homemade cosmetics.

It is said that chewing parsley after drinking alcohol or eating garlic freshens the breath.

ROSEMARY
Rosmarinus officinalis

Long valued as ingredients in cooking, herbal cosmetics, and traditional remedies, the delicate flowers and strongly aromatic leaves of rosemary are ornamental in the herb garden.

Rosemary has spiky aromatic leaves on woody branches. It is a hardy evergreen perennial in most areas, but may need protection in harsh winters. Upright forms can reach 6½ ft (2 m), and the prostrate form spreads and trails. Harvest from growing tips to keep the plant bushy and encourage foliage production. Rosemary flowers in summer, with small aromatic blooms in pink, white, or blue.

R. o. 'Prostratus' is a tender trailing or prostrate form with blue flowers. *R. o.* 'Albus' is hardy and has white flowers. For a tall rosemary hedge, choose *R. o.* 'Miss Jessopp's Upright'. 'Silver Spires' is a rediscovered old rosemary that was popular in Tudor times; it has silvery variegated leaves and is attractive in any season.

This herb prefers a sunny site with a little protection from cold winter winds. Good drainage is essential. Remove any stems that die back in cold weather, and cut back the plant to keep it in shape after flowering.

Use rosemary flowers and chopped young leaves in salads. Rosemary sprigs can be laid on joints of meat before roasting; the leaves may also be added to herbs butters and summer drinks.

SAGE
Salvia officinalis

The classic herb for pork dishes, sage is often combined with applesauce to form one of the best-known partnerships in English cuisine.

Sage has been grown as a medicinal plant since ancient times. The name *Salvia* comes from the Latin *salvere*, meaning to heal, and common sage—known for its astringent qualities—has been widely used as an antiseptic and cleansing herb in remedies and cosmetics. Gargling with a sage infusion can ease the pain of a sore throat.

A hardy evergreen shrub with aromatic and decorative leaves, sage is as versatile in the kitchen as it is ornamental in the flower garden. It is used in numerous meat dishes, sometimes mixed with onion, and in salads, as well as in flavoring salt, oil, and vinegar.

There are many sages that look decorative in flower beds, including *S. o.* 'Tricolor' with leaves variegated in purple, pink, and white. Common sage has grayish-green leaves. Purple or red sage (*S. o.* 'Purpurascens') has purple-gray leaves, while golden sage (*S. o.* 'Icterina') has golden-green leaves.

Sages like full sun, an open site, and light, well-drained soil. Replace plants that become too woody. Take cuttings in spring or mid-fall, or layer branches in situ. Common sage and its varieties can be grown from seed, sown direct into the growing site when danger of frost has passed or in seed trays, cells, or plugs, where temperatures of 60–70°F (16–21°C) will ensure germination after two or three weeks.

SORREL and BUCKLER LEAF SORREL
Rumex acetosa and *Rumex scutatus*

Sorrel is one of the unsung treasures of the herb garden, especially when included in a sauce to serve with oily fish.

Sharp and clean to the taste, sorrel adds piquancy to casseroles and stews. Buckler leaf sorrel (pictured), which has a milder taste, is good in salads or as an alternative to spinach.

One of the traditional herbs of French cuisine, sorrel is an herbaceous perennial that, once established, will be in the herb garden forever. It dies down in winter, but in spring its fresh green leaves appear—and at that time are at their tangy best for use in salads or sauces.

There are two sorrels that are useful in the kitchen and the garden. Common sorrel or garden sorrel (*R. acetosa*) is a strong-growing herb that makes large clumps of shield-shaped leaves, which should be eaten before the plant flowers; tall stems shoot up from the leaf mounds in summer, and the leaves on these stems do not taste as good. Unremarkable small blooms are carried at the ends of the branched flower stems. Of greater attraction in the garden is buckler leaf sorrel or French sorrel (*R. scutatus*). This comes in a green form and a more interesting silver-variegated form, 'Silver Shield,' which has a marbled silvery center to the leaf and gives good ground cover.

Sorrel is valued mainly for its culinary attributes and has been used to treat blood disorders. It has a high oxalic acid content and, if eaten in large quantities, may be harmful, especially to the kidneys—so use with caution.

TARRAGON
Artemisia dracunculus

Tarragon packs a powerful punch in its narrow lancelike leaves. Often teamed with chicken, it is also the herb used to make sauce béarnaise.

The fiery anise flavor of tarragon makes it perfect for spicing meat and fish dishes. The leaves also add piquancy to oils and vinegars, and are excellent in marinades. Pick the leaves during spring and summer to use fresh, and in late summer to freeze for winter use.

French tarragon is a half-hardy perennial with narrow, pale, greenish-gray leaves. It can grow to a height of 60 in (1.5 m) and in summer produces insignificant flowers that never reach maturity. This means that tarragon does not produce viable seed, so it can be propagated only by using root or stem cuttings.

Grow tarragon in light well-drained soil in a sunny site, and cut it back in the fall. Protect the crown with a covering of pine needles or straw during winter. Divide plants in spring or fall.

A less tasty but more vigorous form of the herb is Russian tarragon (*A. dracunculoides*), which is often sold wrongly labeled as French tarragon. This species is very hardy and will survive winters without protection, but it is worth growing French tarragon for its flavor, which is far superior to that of the Russian variety.

Tarragon was once valued as an antidote to snakebite, but has no modern medicinal uses.

THYME
Thymus vulgaris

Both upright and creeping forms of thyme produce aromatic leaves and attractive clusters of small pink, mauve, or white flowers, which are as useful as the foliage in flavoring food.

A hardy evergreen subshrub with small, powerfully aromatic, spike-shaped, or round leaves, thyme is a component of bouquet garni. Both the flowers and the leaves are good in salads and are used to flavor oils, vinegars, and marinades, as well as soups and stews. Thyme is commonly added to stuffing for chickens. It combines well with rosemary.

The most vigorous and most useful for basic flavoring is common thyme (*T. vulgaris*), which has deep-green leaves and is a many-branched woody subshrub. It has mauve flowers. *T. v.* 'Silver Posie' has silver variegated leaves and good flavor. *T.* x *citriodorus* is a shrubby thyme, with small green lemon-scented leaves and pink flowers.

T. x *citriodorus* 'Silver Queen' is variegated with creamy silvery leaves, rosy-pink buds and a strong lemon scent to its leaves. *T. serpyllum* 'Snowdrift' is a creeping thyme that carpets the ground in white when in flower.

The herb is versatile enough to be grown in the garden, in rock gardens, or in containers. The low-growing forms can be used to make attractive flowering paths or fragrant mats at the feet of benches.

Grow thyme in full sun in well-drained soil. After flowering, cut back the plant to promote new growth. Replace plants every few years, when they become too woody and open at their centers.

Thyme has traditionally been used as an antiseptic.

gardening
with herbs

how to grow herbs

Herbs are versatile plants that grow well in most soils and most conditions. They can be increased by dividing plants or taking cuttings. Seed can often be sown where the plants are to grow, also known as "direct sowing." Or you can sow it in pots or seed-starting units, growing the seedlings on a sunny windowsill, under lights, or in a greenhouse.

sowing

Direct-sow the seed of hardy annuals in spring, either in a seedbed or in their growing sites. Half-hardy herbs can also be sown in their growing sites once all danger of frost has passed. Sow the seed in rows and just cover it with soil; water in well and thin out when the seedlings are well established.

Sowing indoors produces plants ready for planting out as soon as the soil warms up and the seedlings have been hardened off in spring.

Almost fill seed trays or pre-formed seed-starting units with soil, firm the surface down, and water the soil, or stand the trays in water. Leave the trays to drain before sowing fine seed into the soil surface. Space out large seeds and sift a thin covering of soil over them. Some types of seed will benefit from bottom heat. Use a heat mat or propagation unit for improved germination. Once the seeds have germinated and are large enough to handle, transplant them into small individual pots.

Harden off the seedlings by leaving them outside during the day and returning them to the greenhouse at night, until they are acclimatized to outdoor conditions. Be sure to increase the exposure to sun gradually.

planting

Before buying an herb that is ready to plant in the yard, check it for disease or pest problems; avoid plants that are root-bound or have damaged stems. Plant the herb as soon as possible, but not during the hottest part of the day. Dig a hole large enough to take the rootball, and remove any weeds from the soil. Put the plant in the hole, backfill with soil, then firm the surface of the soil and water the plant well. In dry conditions water the plant daily until it is well established.

harvesting

Evergreen herbs such as bay, rosemary, sage, and thyme can be harvested from outdoor and indoor herb collections all year around, as can herbs that you have forced into growth in winter, such as mint, tarragon, and chives. Annual herbs, including basil, perilla, rocket, dill,

FROM FAR LEFT **Put a label in place before you sow. Empty the seed packet into your hand and then take a pinch of seed, or one seed if they are large, and place it in a trench or hole. Barely cover the soil and firm it down with the back of your hand. Mark the line of the row with a trail of colored gravel, especially if you are sowing parsley, which is slow to germinate.**

nasturtium, and coriander, are at their best in spring and summer. Since herbaceous perennial herbs including fennel, lovage, and comfrey die back in winter, their harvest period is during the spring and summer. When each plant has produced good leafy growth, harvest it in an even way, to maintain a well-defined shape. For a handful of leaves to add to salads or cooked dishes, pick the herbs just before you want them, at any time of day.

dividing

To promote vigorous growth of perennial herbs or to increase their numbers, divide the plants in early spring when they are still dormant, or in the fall when the growing season is coming to an end. In the fall, before dividing, cut back all old flowering stems. Then use a fork to pry the clump out of the ground. When it is loosened, lift it out and place it on the soil surface.

The traditional way to divide large plants is to place two forks back to back in the center of the clump and pry the two sections of the plant apart. Do this until you have reduced the size of the original clump and produced several new sections ready for replanting. Herbs like chives can be pried apart by hand. Most perennials, such as marjoram, chives, echinacea, tarragon, sorrel, creeping thyme, and lovage, grow to form large basal clumps. The growth at the center weakens, and leaf production usually declines. When the clump is divided, any unhealthy-looking parts can be discarded, which allows the new plant or division to grow healthy new shoots from the rootstock around its edge.

taking cuttings

By taking cuttings from individual plants, you can produce many new plants for your herb garden. You can use a cutting to reproduce exactly the plant from which you have taken the cutting. As soon as the herbs begin to grow in spring, look for strong and healthy new shoots to use as cutting material—these are called softwood cuttings. Cut them away from the parent plant with a sharp knife, and if you are taking several cuttings, put them in a plastic bag to keep them moist and cool, and to prevent them from wilting.

Prepare several pots or trays with a good, well-drained seed-starting mix. Make a clean cut on the stem of each cutting just below a leaf node, so each is 4 in (10 cm) long. Cut the lower leaves off each cutting, but leave a few leaves on the stem. Make holes in the soil with a dibble, and put the cuttings in the holes up to the level of the remaining leaves.

Label each cutting with name and date, then put the pot of cuttings in a heated propagator or a mini-greenhouse made with a plastic bag.

Check cuttings daily; if you are using a plastic bag, take it off and turn it inside out every day When roots start to appear on the underside of the pot—between two and four weeks—you can begin to apply liquid fertilizer. When the plants are large enough, move them to larger pots. Pinch out the growing tips of leafy shoots to encourage a bushy habit.

The method for taking hardwood cuttings is similar to that for taking softwood ones, but hardwood cuttings prefer very well-drained soil, and since they are taken later in the year—in the fall, when the stems are hard and woody— they need to be overwintered in cold frames or greenhouses before planting out the following fall. The rooting time for hardwood cuttings is much longer than for softwood cuttings.

A straightforward way to propagate or increase herbs is to take root cuttings during spring or fall from healthy-looking plants. Mint,

FROM LEFT TO RIGHT
Unless they are in a very large and crowded clump, chives can easily be divided by hand. Dig up and divide the clump by gently pulling it apart. Discard dead or damaged material. Replant smaller clump in prepared planting holes. Backfill and firm in soil at the surface. Trim the tops of the divided plants and water them. Keep the row weed-free, and in a short time you will have a crop of fresh chives.

bergamot, lemon balm, horseradish, comfrey, and sweet woodruff are among the herb plants that can be increased this way.

pests and diseases

Unless they are grown in crowded situations where there is no free circulation of air, or the plants are kept either too wet or too dry, herbs usually remain free of pests and diseases. It is preferable to use organic methods instead of commercial insecticides or fungicides to deter pests from food plants such as herbs. Many organic gardeners use insecticidal soap to get rid of whitefly or greenfly infestations.

Brown spots on mint and chive foliage are symptoms of a disease called mint or onion rust. Plants that are badly affected should be dug up and removed from the bed, so that other plants are not infected. You can also sterilize the soil around mint plants to prevent this disease from occurring: Place a layer of straw around the affected plant and set the straw on fire—but take care to make sure the fire does not spread.

Seedlings of basil and other herbs are prone to damping off and dying in the early stages of growth. Deterrents include good air circulation, hygienic conditions, judicious watering, and drenching the soil with a fungicidal compound before sowing. Scale insects may be a problem on the evergreen leaves of bay grown in containers indoors. Use a soapy liquid to wipe the leaves, and dislodge the scale insects with the end of a cotton swab.

Vine weevil, whitefly, and red spider mites may be persistent in protected environments, but can be controlled with insecticidal soap or biological controls. Eelworms or nematodes are used for vine weevil, a parasitic wasp called *Encarsia formosa* for whitefly, and *Phytoseiulus persimilis* for red spider mites.

beautiful beds

Many of the plants categorized as herbs are attractive flowering or foliage plants that can be taken out of the context of the herb garden and used successfully in a mixed bed.

Sage—whose foliage colors range from silver to purple, and include a tricolor variety that is gray-green with hints of pink and white—is a particularly effective bedding plant. Sage grows to form a low mass of colored foliage, so it can be useful at the base of plants such as roses, which may have bare stems. Later in the season, when it flowers itself, sage offers extra ornament. Once the flowers have faded, cut back the plant to prevent it from becoming leggy and out of shape and to encourage the continuous production of foliage.

If you can accommodate their invasive habits, herbs such as mint, comfrey, and sweet cicely will provide good-textured, colorful, and shapely foliage followed by pretty flowers. All three are useful in shady sites, with mint being suited to moister conditions. Borage is another vigorous but useful foliage plant that bears eye-catching blue or white flowers in summer.

Johnny-jump-ups, with their small mauve "faces," are useful in containers as well as at the front of a bed, winding their way through other plants. Their silver foliage and dainty pink

ABOVE LEFT **Mauve marjoram graces the front of a flower bed, while evening primrose, chicory, and fennel offer tall stems of flowers in yellow and blue, white, or (in some species of chicory) pink, which gives the impression of floating high in the air.**

LEFT **Starlike blue chicory looks delicately beautiful en masse, as well as in a mixed planting.**

RIGHT **Curry plant and lavender grow in curved shapes, which makes their silver-gray foliage useful for softening the edges of beds.**

LEFT Echinacea is a native American herb with a long medicinal tradition. It has many potential uses in modern medicine, and is constantly being assessed for its potential benefits to the human immune system. In the flower bed, it offers attractive long-lasting blooms late in the season.

OPPOSITE, ABOVE
Boxwood trained into formal shapes is a useful accent in a mixed bed. Marjoram and bee balm, or monarda, bring a lovely combination of foliage and flowers to the bed.

OPPOSITE, BELOW
Calendula, or pot marigolds, will brighten a sunny bed in spring and early summer. To encourage a continuity of flowering, remove the old flowers before they set seed.

or white scented blooms make pinks suitable for low-growing at the front of the flower bed. Similarly, thyme will provide variegated gold or silver foliage, delicate white, mauve, or pink blooms and, in some cases, a low-growing habit.

Oregano or marjoram is a rewarding herb for the middle or front of a flower bed, and will grow to form fairly large clumps of flowering stems in white or mauve.

Most herb flowers are in the mauve, pink, or white ranges, but plants such as fennel, calendula, with its sunny orange and creamy yellow flowers, and nasturtium, in shades of orange, cream, and red, provide great swaths of color in the mixed bed. Nasturtiums have the added advantage of colorful foliage and look good weaving their way along the front of the bed. St. John's wort can be used to add spots of buttery yellow to the front of a bed, complementing evening primrose in a similar shade at the back; both herbs self-seed copiously, so cut them back once the blooms are finished.

At a slightly higher level, fennel's early offering to the bed is a froth of ferny foliage in either green or bronze, followed by stiff upside-down umbrellalike flower heads with masses of small yellow dotlike flowers. These are a magnet for beneficial garden insects such as hoverflies, and because fennel self-seeds abundantly around the garden, at the height of summer it offers great stands of color, seemingly dancing with life.

Lavender, pinks, and some other herbs grow in soft mounded shapes that spill over the edge of the bed. Others, such as chicory, offer flowering stems that seem to float through other plants in the bed. Rosemary and bay are useful grown as standards in formal gardens, serving to raise eye-level and to make a repeated theme along a long bed.

In late summer, traditional herb-garden plants, such as echinacea, or purple coneflower (also available in a white and a green form), are useful because they flower for a long time late in the season. Bee balm, or monarda, has a similarly long and late flowering season, and provides tall stems of flowers arranged in whorls of mauve, white, and pink around its square stems. Hyssop, with mauve-and-white flower spikes, is also useful for the middle of the late-summer bed.

covering the ground

Many low-growing herbs are ideal in the ornamental garden
as groundcovering plants. Creeping thyme, for example,
makes a flat green mat of foliage, and in summer offers its
small mauve blooms for extra show. In a bed it hugs the
ground at the feet of taller plants, suppressing weeds and
providing its own color. Deadhead thyme after flowering,
using shears or clippers. Remove any weed seedlings that
grow through the groundcover and water it in dry spells.
Since it supports light foot traffic, thyme can be used for a
short path. More formally, it makes a witty feature planted
in a circle at the base of a sundial.

Creeping chamomile is useful as a fragrant groundcover, to
create an aromatic lawn or as a path plant. Remove perennial
weeds and stones from the soil before planting. For 1 square
yard (1 square meter), you will need 40 individual chamomile
plants. Water them in well, and don't walk on the lawn or
path until they are established and have meshed together.

Either thyme or chamomile makes a fragrant cover for a
grass seat or bench. Site the seat against a wall and make a
back for it with trellis or wood. You can build up the seat in
front of it as you would a raised bed, using smaller raised
beds to form the "arms" of the seat. Plant the creeping
herbs in the soil within the various raised areas and, if you
are using trellis for the back, plant a climber such as jasmine
into the bed, for fragrance in the air and at your back.

Prostrate rosemary, although it is slower growing than
thyme and chamomile, and tender in cold areas, is effective
both as a groundcover and trailing over the edges of beds.
Plant in full sun. Corsican mint, *Mentha requienii*, won't
support feet, but makes a good cover at the edge of a pond
or in a moist, shady conditions. Similarly, creeping mint,
M. pulegium, is attractive in a shady, slightly damp area of
the yard. Herbs such as *Alchemilla mollis*, sweet cicely, and
salad burnet, although not ground-hugging, are useful
groundcover plants in a large yard. They self-seed abundantly,
so their spread can be prodigious.

LEFT Two types of thyme form the groundcover that frames pots holding lemon verbena and an ornamental garden plant, Perovskia 'Blue Spire.'

ABOVE AND RIGHT Creeping thyme (above) or chamomile (right) wears better when grown between stepping stones. Either herb supports light traffic and makes a highly aromatic path to a bench or an arbor. Both need to be clipped back to stop them from covering the stepping stones.

a hedge of herbs

Rosemary, thyme, santolina, boxwood, and lavender are among the herbs that can be grown as shaped low hedges to enclose formal features or even to form the fabric of herb parterres. Herb hedges are usually shaped to make linear ribbons of foliage that outline or emphasize special areas of an herb garden. Yew may be slow-growing, but once established, it is a very elegant dark-green foil for herbs, and useful as an architectural hedge plant.

Knot gardens and parterres are the usual formal features created with herbs. The color of the hedge depends on the plants you choose for it. For a silvery effect, use lavender, santolina, or curry plant. Thyme, rosemary, and boxwood provide green elements, and by mixing the silver and greens you can create a woven effect.

While keeping lavender closely clipped gives a formal effect, letting it flower in summer, then cutting it back once the flowering is finished, creates a relaxed and informal look. A lavender hedge makes an attractive feature on each side of a path, but make the area wide enough to allow the lavender spikes to spill across it while leaving enough space for you to walk along.

When you plant an herb hedge, use plants of the same height and size to achieve a uniform look more quickly. Plant boxwood or yew in individual planting holes along a line of string. Water the plants in well and, if necessary, provide a temporary windbreak of burlap to help young plants survive their first winter.

When the hedge is well established, you can begin to clip it to maintain it. Cut back knot-garden or parterre hedges in the early fall, so there is time for them to recover before the cold

ABOVE **After lavender has finished flowering, cut it back to a uniform height for a fragrant hedge.**

RIGHT **Cotton lavender or santolina can be grown to achieve a silvery effect.**

OPPOSITE **A circle of wall germander is created from single plants of the same size planted in a particular design, then cut back each year to the desired shape.**

weather sets in. Woody plants such as sage, thyme, lavender, and rosemary should be cut back to half the year's growth to promote bushy shapes. For extra effect, cut special shapes, such as triangles, globes, or even whimsical animals or birds, into the hedges.

herbs in the vegetable garden

Growing popular culinary herbs such as parsley and chives as crops in the vegetable garden means you can harvest several plants at the same time rather than one or two—so each plant loses some of its foliage, flowers, or seeds, but enough remains for the plant to stay decorative and viable.

Group tall plants such as fennel and lovage together and plant them at the back of the vegetable garden so they don't cast shade or take light away from lower-growing herbs. Low-growing herbs such as parsley, salad burnet, chives, and buckler leaf sorrel look good in short rows in raised beds.

Sow parsley in succession through the summer so you have several rows at different stages. Once parsley begins to send up a strong, tough flowering stem its foliage becomes less aromatic, and you should uproot the plants. In an informal vegetable garden, allow one plant to flower and set seed, and then to self-seed.

Summer savory, an annual with tasty edible flowers and foliage, has traditionally been cooked and served with beans; it is also often used as a companion plant for beans in the vegetable garden. Another good companion herb is sweet cicely, traditionally linked

with one of the early fruits of the productive garden, rhubarb. Use its leafy shoots to reduce the acidity of rhubarb. Sweet cicely self-sows copiously, so remove its seeds once they have formed or harvest them to use as anise-flavored sweets.

Mint is useful in salads and in cooked dishes, sauces, and jellies. It is a vigorous plant best grown in pots sunk into the ground or in a section of the vegetable garden that can be cordoned off from the rest of the rows. Although its flowers are attractive, keep cutting out flowering stems to encourage more leafy shoots.

Cut back thyme and sage after flowering to promote the growth of new leafy shoots. Rosemary also benefits from cutting back. Some woody herbs become leggy and unshapely in time. If this happens, replace them with new plants.

Grow golden marjoram and chervil in relative shade. Chervil is a biennial producing leafy growth in its first year, so make successive sowings to keep your kitchen supplied with its subtle flavors.

Herbs such as nasturtium, johnny-jump-ups, and calendula provide edible flowers for use in salads. Chive flower heads are also good in salads—pick them just as the buds begin to open.

OPPOSITE, TOP ROW
Confine vigorous mint (left) in a restricted area of the vegetable garden. Rosemary (center) can be clipped into shapes or allowed to grow freely. Use flat-leaved parsley (right) as a seasonal edging.

OPPOSITE, BOTTOM ROW
Harvest the aromatic seeds of caraway (left) after the flowers die back. Curly-leaved parsley (center) can also be used as temporary edging. The flowers, foliage, and seeds of nasturtium (right) are spicy in food—and it will romp through the vegetable garden, providing annual color.

creating an herb collection

If you have space to grow herbs for ornament, display them in groups according to their use or to show the differences between plants in the same genus.

There are herbs for every theme and color scheme. For example, collections of mint, rosemary, thyme, lavender, marjoram, and sage reveal a wide range of foliage color, flower color and, in many cases, essential oils and aromas. Such collections, arranged by genus and species, show off the characteristics of the various plants and display the differences between each species and form.

Before you plant a collection, you need to know the maximum heights and spreads of the various plants and how much sun they need. Look at the different foliage colors and place them so they look good together.

The simplest collection consists of the herbs you use often in the kitchen. Grow them in a small circular bed or in containers close to the kitchen door for easy access. You could devote a small rectangular bed to bay, thyme, and parsley, the three classic herbs of a bouquet garni. Choose a standard or conical-shaped bay as the central focus. Plant

TOP Mints are best grown in individual pots to prevent these vigorous plants from overwhelming each other.

ABOVE Rosemary flowers can be white, pink, mauve, or blue. Most species are medium-height, but 'Miss Jessopp's Upright,' which can grow to 8 ft (2.5 m), needs careful siting in such a collection.

RIGHT AND OPPOSITE A circle is a popular shape for a basic culinary collection containing herbs such as rosemary, chives, marjoram, and buckler leaf sorrel.

thyme in the corners of the bed, and fill the center with parsley. For a *fines herbes* collection, grow parsley, chervil, chives, and tarragon. If you have a fondness for Italian cuisine, grow bay, basil, marjoram, garlic, rosemary, and sage. For an Asian taste, choose cilantro, lemongrass, mitsuba, perilla, and mint. Pizza herb gardens containing marjoram, basil, basil, and rosemary are also popular.

You could also group together herbs whose leaves are commonly used dried or fresh to make teas and tisanes, such as sage, mint, bergamot, and chamomile. Other possibilities range from fragrant herbs for a potpourri collection to an edible flower collection. Enjoy cowslip and violet flowers crystallized or baked in cakes and scones. Use calendula, chive, and thyme flowers fresh in salads. Lavender flowers and rose petals added to ordinary or superfine sugar will transform it into a scented sweetener for baking and desserts.

The many herbs that have citrus-scented foliage would make an attractive collection with their differing heights, shapes, foliage, and flower colors. Such plants include variegated lemon balm, lemon verbena, lemon thyme, and some tender herbs such as lemon-scented basil, lemongrass, and lemon-scented gum.

LEFT **Several different thyme species are grown within a small parterre or knot garden, hedged in by rosemary, box, and a golden form of the honeysuckle** *Lonicera nitida*, **'Baggessen's Gold,' a shrubby hedge plant.**

RIGHT **Edging an informal path with collections of marjoram and catmint offers a flowing, curving shape to the garden and displays differences in flower color.**

herbs in containers

There are many low-growing or trailing herbs that grow well in containers, and using containers makes it simple to replace old herbs quickly as particular plants reach the end of their productive life or as different varieties become available during the course of the season.

The most convenient containers for kitchen herbs are windowboxes placed just outside the kitchen—so you can harvest foliage and flowers easily and quickly without having to step outside—or large ground-level containers on a patio.

If any of the herbs in a container dies, or you harvest them so completely that they are no longer attractive, it is simple to remove and replace them. In addition, if you will be using and replacing the herbs regularly, you can leave them in their individual containers, all set into a sturdy wooden windowbox, with the box becoming a cachepot for the various smaller containers. You can replace any herb that is not growing well without having to replant the whole box.

There is a wide variety of different containers that are suitable for herb growing. Terra cotta and plastic are popular choices, but you can use almost anything, from large olive-oil cans to half-barrels, to create a particular style and house your herb collection.

There are two things you need to be sure of when planting a container with herbs. First, the container should have a depth of at least 10–12 in (25–30 cm), to give the roots plenty of space to make strong root runs. Second, larger containers are heavy to move once they are full of moist soil, so you need to put them in an

LEFT **Terra-cotta pots are attractive containers for herbs because they weather so well. Annual herbs and some perennials, including chives, thrive in small pots in the short term. Woody perennials such as sage and thyme need relatively deep pots so their roots can get properly established.**

appropriate location before you plant. If you are planting a windowbox or hanging basket, make sure it is anchored securely in position. When it is full of moist soil it will be very heavy, and if it became unsecured, it could fall and hurt someone passing underneath it, especially if you happen to live in an apartment.

Remove the individual herbs from the pots in which they came from the nursery and place them on a drainage layer of broken terra cotta and a layer of potting soil. Fill the spaces between the herbs with soil and firm the plants in with your hands. Water the soil and cover its surface with a layer of grit to hold the soil in place and to act as a mulch.

There are a number of herbs that will thrive growing together in a container in a sunny situation. Avoid tall-growing plants—especially for a windowbox where the window opens out—because they will flop over the edge and may be damaged by wind.

BELOW AND BELOW RIGHT **Weathered stone sinks or sculpted terra-cotta pots are practical and attractive containers for shrubby herbs like sage. They are also good for low-growing** collections of creeping and upright thymes.

ABOVE Thyme and sage combine well in a basket with ornamental plants such as trailing verbena.

LEFT **Standard bay trees make strong focal points in a formal herb garden. In winter, insulate the pot with bubblewrap to prevent frost damage and stabilize it so it doesn't blow over.**

OPPOSITE PAGE **A bold, flamboyant display in a container can be used as a marker for the meeting point of paths or to provide a change of height in a low-growing herb garden.**

growing herbs indoors

Many herbs can be grown indoors throughout the year, but indoor herbs are especially useful during winter for quick harvesting. In sheltered sites they can also be grown on patios and balconies in winter. Treat indoor herbs as practical or useful plants with short shelf or windowsill lives rather than as long-lived plants. Like other container-grown plants, they need nutrients, water, protection from pests, adequate light, and free circulation of air.

A kitchen windowsill is usually the best site for herbs in pots because it is convenient for the cook and is likely to have good light and air circulation. Choose attractive containers for a decorative effect, or group several herbs in large containers to create a mini-herb garden indoors.

As a rule, grow herbs in separate pots in well-drained soil to allow for easy replacement of dead or over-harvested herbs. Water the plants regularly, but in winter keep rosemary, sage, winter savory, and thyme just moist.

Herbs grown indoors in summer need a liquid feed every two to three weeks—or add a slow-release granular fertilizer to the soil when you pot the plants. Use a spray of insecticidal soap to kill off aphids; spray every 14 days until the infestation has abated. Harvest from the herbs as required, but turn each plant every few days to encourage even leaf growth and to help you harvest evenly from it. If you over-harvest from one plant it will look less attractive and may become more vulnerable to pests and diseases.

For quick results, replace indoor plants with new ones bought from supermarkets; for a longer growing period, replace them with herbs from garden centers. You can sow parsley and

chervil in succession to provide new material. Evergreen herbs, such as rosemary, sage, and thyme, grow well indoors. Annuals such as basil and parsley last for a short time, but replacement pots can be bought regularly from supermarkets for immediate use.

If you have no garden and are growing herbs in pots indoors all year around, repot evergreen perennials annually in spring. The plants may need replacing every two or three years. Plants such as fennel and dill, which would normally grow very tall outdoors, should be harvested when they are reasonably short, or the plant will become leggy and look untidy and out of line with its windowsill companions.

If you have a heated greenhouse, you can force tarragon, mint, and chives into growing during what would normally be their dormant season. Put them in pots in the fall and keep them in the greenhouse through the winter, planting them in the yard in spring.

Container herbs can be bought from supermarkets at any time of the year to fill the flavor gap between your own sowings and provide leaves for salads and cooked dishes. The hothouse conditions in which they are grown are difficult to replicate in the average drafty kitchen, but you can prolong their lives by keeping them out of drafts, watering them from the base and harvesting them evenly. Even if you are careful with them, it is unlikely that supermarket plants will become long-term inhabitants of your indoor collection.

Supermarkets can also be a source of unusual herbs for indoors. For example, lemongrass plants can be grown from stems bought in supermarket packs. (In some Asian stores, they are sold loose.) Choose the plumpest stem and check that it has not been sliced at the base. Plant the stem in gritty soil and keep it on the dry side during winter. Alternatively, good-sized plants are available from specialized herb growers and will provide citrus-scented foliage much earlier than the supermarket stems.

LEFT **Fennel, parsley, basil, and sage will grow well on a sunny windowsill, but they need to be kept out of drafts. Fennel tends to become leggy if it is grown indoors in a container, so use it quickly.**

living with herbs

To create a warm welcome, bring the essence of a summer garden indoors with a potpourri of flowers, herbs, and spices.

The original "rotten pot" that gave us the word potpourri was a wet mixture of fermented petals and leaves. Today, the dry potpourri is more popular. Its scent may not last as long as that of its predecessor, but the combinations of textures, colors, and aromas are endless. The basic ingredients are flowers for scent or color, aromatic leaves, peel, and spices, and a fixative—usually powdered orris root—to preserve the blend. Use 1 tablespoon of orris root for each cupped handful of dried flowers and leaves; then add a few drops of essential oils, if desired.

ABOVE AND OPPOSITE **For a zesty hallway, add essential oils of bergamot, grapefruit, and lemon to a bowl of dried lemon balm, lemon verbena, mint, yellow rosebuds, and citrus slices. Any essential oil must be used sparingly or it will drown the subtler scents of the leaves and petals. The potpourri in this shallow bowl—about the size of a dinner plate—needs no more than 2 drops of each oil.**

RIGHT **To enhance the rustic feeling in a room with plenty of wooden furniture, mix 2 or 3 drops of essential oils of pine, sandalwood, and cedar with large handfuls of dried rose petals, bay leaves, and lavender sprigs, along with generous sprinklings of ground cinnamon and nutmeg.**

Designed for relaxation, comfort and entertaining, living rooms are full of textiles and display surfaces that offer a host of opportunities for scenting and decorating with herbs.

A simple way to scent your home is to have arrangements of fresh flowers and herbs in each room, but there are more imaginative ways to keep it smelling delicious all year round.

For example, herb sachets—which have traditionally been used to freshen drawers and linen cupboards—can also be tucked into pillows, into the pockets of everyday coats and clothes, and down the sides of comfortable chairs and sofas. Fragrances are released when herb-filled cushions are pressed or leaned against; curtain hems can be filled with dried aromatic herbs, or fresh lavender sprigs can simply be tucked into voile curtains. Experiment with different mixtures of dried herbs and essential oils to make a potpourri, perhaps combining it with a pomander. Circulating air will pick up and mingle these scents, so make sure the various fragrances are complementary, and there is no clash of pungent odors.

For a sweet aroma, choose from herbs that sweeten, which include bay, lavender, lemon verbena, rosemary, santolina, myrtle, and thyme.

ABOVE LEFT AND OPPOSITE **Herb sachets can become a decorative element in themselves, while subtly perfuming an entire room—the perfect setting in which to enjoy a cup of chamomile tea.**

ABOVE RIGHT **For a heady winter fragrance, press cloves into oranges to make pomanders. Display several in a dish with herbs and spices such as bay, eucalyptus, juniper berries, and cinnamon.**

Pocketing a subtle perfume

A pocket in a pillow invites you to fill it with herbs. Herbs that are good for this purpose include eucalyptus (opposite page), rosemary and bay leaves. For a mixture of herbs, whole or crushed, cut a square of gauze and fold it to make an envelope around the herbs (this page). Wrap a band of linen around a pillow, securing the ends with a button or a stitch. Tuck the folded gauze sachet under the band. Essential oils sprinkled on the gauze bag enhance and prolong the fragrance.

BELOW **You can buy ready-scented beeswax candles, or add essential oils or small pieces of dried herb to melted beeswax while making your own. Tied up in ribbon with lavender sprigs, they make beautiful handmade Christmas presents.**

A handful of woody sprigs on a log fire intensifies the smoky aromas of winter.

ABOVE RIGHT AND OPPOSITE **If you have a log fire, throw on a handful of woody-stemmed herbs every now and again to release the rich aromas. Layering logs with branches of rosemary both looks pretty and complements the woody smells.**

Burning woody herbs such as rosemary, lavender, and bay will fill a room with rich musty aromas. Either keep a box of dried herbs beside an open fire to use as kindling, or throw an occasional handful on the embers. Layer logs stored in the home with generous sprigs of rosemary (drying the rosemary beforehand should stop it from turning black).

Another delicious winter fragrance is the smell of burning candles. To create your own herbal version, buy a candle-making kit. Just before pouring the melted wax into molds, add small pieces of dried herb, such as bergamot, wall germander, lavender heads, lemon thyme, mint, rosemary, or myrtle, or a few drops of essential oil of your choice.

Flamboyant winter wreaths enhance a Yuletide mood.

A traditional ways to use herbs for decoration is to weave them into a wreath. This adds fragrance and color to a room and can become the central focus. The wreath shown on these pages is a strong enough statement to be the only festive decoration in the room.

To make a wreath, use plain wire, moss-covered wire, or willow, and secure into a hoop. (Or buy a hoop ready-made from a florist.) Using thin wire, attach bunches of selected herbs. For the main body of the wreath, use branches of pine, rosemary, eucalyptus, and bay; then carefully tuck in among the branches slices of dried lemons, oranges, and limes, fresh or dried Chinese lanterns, and bundles of cinnamon sticks. For a final festive touch, add bunches of red berries.

To hang the wreath horizontally, attach it to a strong structure such as the iron candelabra illustrated. When it is no longer needed, burn the bunches of herbs on an open fire and enjoy the powerful aroma.

LEFT AND RIGHT **A wreath of pine branches, eucalyptus, rosemary, bay, slices of dried citrus fruit, and bundles of cinnamon sticks will fill a room with a distinctively festive mixture of colors, textures, and fragrances.**

Generous bunches of dried herbs, or herbs preserved in attractive bottles of oil or vinegar, can be used in the kitchen for decorative as well as culinary purposes.

The still room for processing and preserving herbs, which dated from medieval times, has long since disappeared from the home. Such activities now often take place in the kitchen, where herbs may also be stored, grown (see pages 54–55), or used decoratively.

As soon as possible after harvesting or buying herbs, put them in water and out of direct sunlight. To revive cooking herbs that are starting to wilt, put them in a plastic bag filled with air and secure it tightly; stored in the refrigerator, they should last a few extra days.

The sooner after harvesting the drying process begins, the better the quality and color of the dried herbs, but drying cannot be rushed because moisture must be removed gradually from a plant. Wipe off any soil or grit, but avoid washing the leaves. Choose a warm, dry, dark

place with good ventilation, such as a heated attic. Hang several sprigs of each herb in separate small bunches, tied loosely with string or raffia, so the air can get in and around each bunch. Leave herbs hanging, stems upward, for about a week, until the leaves are paper-dry and fragile, but not disintegrating. Remove leaves from stems, keeping them whole, and store in airtight bottles away from sunlight.

Check dried leaves regularly for moisture, mold, and insects, and throw them away if you find anything wrong. Most dried herbs will last for about a year.

Freezing is an excellent way to retain the color and flavor of delicate herbs such as basil, chives, dill, and tarragon. Before freezing, wipe the herbs and pack them into labelled plastic food bags or boxes.

ABOVE LEFT **To dry herbs, tie a few sprigs together and hang them in a warm, dark room.**

ABOVE **Store herb oils and vinegars in airtight bottles out of direct sunlight.**

RIGHT **Hanging herbs from the ceiling can produce a dramatic decorative effect. Fragrant bunches of sage, lemon balm, rosemary, and eucalyptus, dried or fresh, are bound to brighten up and invigorate any kitchen.**

RIGHT The acrid smell of rue repels flies and ants. Hang up bunches of rue in utility rooms to discourage infestations, and press the leaves from time to time to release their pungent scent.

BELOW Pretty posies of santolina in your linen drawers will ward off the dreaded moth.

LEFT **To give a wonderfully fresh fragrance to floors and surfaces, clean them with 6 drops of an essential oil in a quart (2 liters) of warm water. Choose from oils of lemon, lavender, tea tree, sandalwood, thyme, peppermint, and eucalyptus.**

RIGHT **To make your wooden furniture smell dreamy, add a few drops of essential oil of lavender to good-quality beeswax furniture polish, and apply with a clean dry cloth.**

Herbs have always had a practical role in the household, and that remains true today—indeed, incorporating herbs or essential herbal oils in your cleaning routine can make household chores an aromatic pleasure.

You can use them to disinfect floors and surfaces, to repel unwanted visitors such as moths and other insects, and to sweeten and purify stale, musty air.

Sprigs of pennyroyal, rue, and tansy left on pantry shelves will see off ants. Rue will also deter flies, as will mint, mugwort, pennyroyal, peppermint, and lavender. Use the herbs dried in potpourri, or fresh in arrangements and wreaths. Disturb the leaves occasionally to release more scent.

To deter weevils, place a few bay leaves in canisters of flour, rice, and dried legumes.

Herbal preparations have a multitude of practical uses in the home—and they are frequently kinder to your skin and the environment than chemical-based cleaners.

ABOVE **Roses, Chinese lanterns, and pelargoniums add color to a summer garland of flat-leaved parsley, bay, lemon balm, coriander, fennel, apple mint, eucalyptus, and sage.**

RIGHT **In addition to making great centerpieces, fresh herbs can be used for plate decorations, in finger bowls, and in place-marker pots.**

FAR RIGHT **Leaves of borage and mint with cucumber slices make iced water even more refreshing. Coriander flowers impart a delicate flavor to pepper and salt.**

Decorating a summer table with fresh herbs is a joy in itself. There is such a wide choice of plants and flowers available in summer that each detail can be a celebration of a different herb. For example, wrapping flowering rosemary around napkins will encourage your guests to appreciate the plant's delicate purple flower.

For your tablecloth, choose a pale natural fabric such as undyed linen. This will allow the herbs to occupy center stage rather than making them compete with a busy pattern. Height is important in any table setting; one easy way to achieve it is to decorate candelabra or candlesticks. Soak a foam brick in water. (These can be bought from florists and, if kept damp, will keep the herbs fresh for days.) Slice off two chunks, one for each side of the candlestick, and use floral tape to wrap them together. Rosemary, eucalyptus, lemon balm, parsley, flowering apple mint, and various pelargoniums make a good base. You can then introduce more delicate herbs and flowers

Intensify the pleasures of summer dining by combining the delicate scents of freshly cut flowers and herbs with the stronger aromas of herbs used in cooking and the spicy flavors of salad herbs.

Each place setting is adorned with a herbal napkin ring, a finger bowl sprinkled with aromatic herbs, and a miniature pot of herbs that acts as a holder for placecards.

such as flowering coriander and old-fashioned scented roses. Combining culinary herbs and scent-giving herbs in a table decoration can produce extremely satisfying results, especially if the culinary herbs have also been used in the preparation of food.

A bowl of freshly torn or chopped herbs such as basil, mint, tarragon, cilantro, and flat-leaved parsley is an attractive detail—and will allow your guests to help themselves to handfuls to sprinkle on their food.

As with the tablecloth, choose plain or understated china, flatware, and glassware that will not upstage the greenery. Arrange the herbs loosely; think about how they grow in the garden and let them ramble across the table.

OPPOSITE, LEFT **A sprig of rosemary tied loosely around a crisp linen napkin is an original and attractive alternative to a napkin ring.**

OPPOSITE, RIGHT **Lemon balm's woody stems are easy to weave into lattice-pattern placemats. When a hot plate is put on a mat, a delicious aroma is released.**

ABOVE **Float leaves of mint and lemon balm in bowls of water to allow your visitors to rinse their fingers between courses.**

ABOVE RIGHT **Write the names of your guests on copper plant tags and put them in miniature terra cotta plant pots filled with fresh herbs.**

Herbs wilt quickly, so make sure they are in plenty of water. Spray loose herbs with water half an hour before your guests sit down, to keep the table looking fresh.

If you have a conservatory to dine in, or if your dining room is full of natural light, take advantage of this environment to grow herbs in containers (see pages 54–55). Surround the table with pots of delicious-smelling culinary and aromatic herbs. For containers that are intended to be a permanent feature, choose unusual items such as china basins and chimney pots. Trailing herbs in hanging baskets make romantic decorations; suitable varieties include prostrate rosemary, prostrate sage, creeping thymes, catnip, and the colorful nasturtium.

Although they may seem out of place in an office, herbs can do much to enhance your working environment. Particular varieties of herb have been shown to invigorate and uplift the mind, aiding concentration and inspiration. Keep a pot of fresh herbs on your desk or near your work area, where the leaves and flowers will be lovely to look at and will gently fragrance the air.

Essential oils sprinkled onto a tissue or handkerchief are an alternative to fresh herbs and provide a stronger herbal "hit." Basil is energizing and invigorating, and is used to treat depression. Cilantro and eucalpytus are also uplifting. Geranium is refreshing and relaxing, as is lavender. Lemon balm bursts with zingy fragrance, and thyme is effective at combating fatigue and depression.

Even the paper you use can be scented—either buy it ready-scented or add a few drops of essential oil. Stick dried herbs to paper or leave them loose in a folded letter. A sophisticated flower press is not needed. Simply take a perfect flower or leaf and sandwich it between two piles of blotting or watercolor paper. Put this sandwich between the leaves of a large heavy book and pile three or four more heavy books on top of it. Leave for a couple of weeks, until the herbs have dried out.

Ink, too, can be fragranced. Immerse 1 oz. (25 g) of dried aromatic flowers (such as myrtle, lavender flowers, lemon verbena, pelargonium, or rosemary) in water and bring to a boil. Simmer for 30–40 minutes until it has reduced to about 4 teaspoons of pungent dark liquid. Strain, let it cool, and add to a bottle of ordinary ink.

ABOVE **As a powerful aid to concentration, place a pitcher of fresh herbs such as basil and mint on a desk in a work space.**

LEFT **Writing paper can be scented with a few drops of essential oil and decorated with dried pressed herbs. Even the ink you use to write a letter can be fragranced.**

Refreshing and invigorating herbs can bring a new sense of purpose to your working space, and revive some of the almost forgotten pleasures of letter writing.

LEFT **Herbs with colorful and pretty blooms can be dried and pressed the same way as any wildflowers before being incorporated into eye-catching arrangements.**

Fragrant nosegays and tussie-mussies were traditionally associated with declarations of love or used to ward off dangerous diseases.

LEFT **This tussie-mussie includes flowering thyme for courage, fennel for strength, lemon balm for sympathy, and geranium for comfort.**

RIGHT **A bridal bed decorated with fresh flowering thyme, rosemary, pelargoniums, eucalyptus, and roses looks romantic and will fill a room with fresh summer smells.**

Nosegays or tussie-mussies—posies made up of aromatic herbs and flowers—were popular from medieval times not only because of their ability to disguise unpleasant smells but also because they were thought to protect the holder from serious diseases.

They were also used for declarations of love, since all the flowers and herbs had special meanings. A lover might send a posy of, for example, mint for virtue, forget-me-nots for true love, golden marjoram for blushes, myrtle for love, rosemary for remembrance and ivy for fidelity.

Guests will be sure to appreciate such a posy placed on a pillow or at the bedside, even if they have no idea of the signficance of the herbs and flowers used.

To fill a bedroom with summer scent in winter, spray bed linen with a fresh linen spray or sprinkle pillows with a diluted essential oil. Chamomile, lavender, lemon balm, and oregano have been shown to promote sound sleep. Another way to scent a room in winter, when fresh herbs are scarce,

Garland your home to make life sweeter.

ABOVE **Catnip's long woody stems can be looped into a fresh herbal garland.**

ABOVE RIGHT **Its strength and pliability make dried lavender ideal for bending and weaving into shape.**

is to vaporize an essential herbal oil in a ceramic burner. Add a few drops of oil to water in the bowl and use a nightlight to heat it gently from beneath.

Garlands serve the same purpose as potpourri. They are designed to scent the air and the objects around them, but in a more decorative way. They can be hung on the backs of doors or on bed corners, or placed on a pillow to welcome a guest. Only herbs with tough and pliable stems can be used to make garlands because they must be able to withstand being looped and twisted. For fresh herbal garlands use catmint, lemon balm, lemon verbena, marjorams, mints, and scented pelargoniums. Rosemary, lavender, bay, myrtle, and eucalpytus are rewarding to use in either fresh or dried form.

THIS PAGE **The scent of lavender has a relaxing effect and promotes sound sleep, so it is a particularly appropriate herb for decorative use in the bedroom.**

An aromatic herbal bath is one of the most pleasurable ways to cleanse your skin and revitalize your whole body. You can add herbs to promote relaxation or stimulation.

ABOVE **Put a bar of herbal soap on a bed of fresh mint. An invigorating aroma is released when the leaves are gently crushed.**

ABOVE CENTER **Hang a bunch of fresh herbs from the hot-water faucet before the tub is filled with water. Lemon balm and eucalyptus have a revitalizing effect in the morning.**

LEFT AND ABOVE RIGHT **Scatter fresh lavender around the tub and put down a cotton mat to stand on. The scent of crushed lavender fills the room and permeates nearby spaces.**

Some herbs invigorate; others soothe the mind and body. For stimulation, choose basil, bay, rosemary, eucalyptus, lemon verbena, mint, sage, and thyme. For relaxation, go for chamomile, lavender, and lemon balm. To treat minor skin irritations or to soothe dry and sensitive skin, use calendula, comfrey, fennel, lady's mantle, parsley, and spearmint.

Any of these herbs can be used, in dried form, in a herbal bath. The herbs should be crushed or ground and put into a gauze bag; hang the bag under a hot faucet before filling the tub. The water should be close to body temperature; if it is too hot, the skin perspires and fails to take advantage of the therapeutic qualities. To enjoy the full benefits of the bath, wallow in it for at least 10 minutes. See the next page for therapeutic herbal preparations to make at home.

lavender spritz

For a classic skin freshener, fill an atomizer bottle with distilled water and add a couple of drops of lavender oil. Shake to blend.

hand cream

1 cup (250 ml) rosewater
¼ cup (60 ml) glycerin
¼ cup (60 ml) cornstarch
3 drops chamomile oil

Blend rosewater, cornstarch, and glycerin. Heat gently in a double boiler to thicken, then cool. Stir in oil. Store in screw-top jar.

lip balm

Oil of eucalyptus, lemon, thyme, jasmine, lavender, geranium, juniper, or peppermint

Add 2 drops of an oil to 1 tablespoon of warmed cocoa butter. Put in a small jar and let it cool.

rosewater toner

⅔ cup (150 ml) rosewater
⅔ cup (150 ml) witch hazel
6 drops glycerin

Pour all the ingredients into a bottle and shake well before use.

vinegar bath

Boil leaves of lemon balm and pennyroyal in cider vinegar. Infuse overnight, then strain. Pour into warm water for a refreshing bath.

massage oil

5 drops lavender oil
5 drops neroli oil
6 drops frankincense
¼ cup (60 ml) almond oil

Add oils to a small stoppered jar and shake to blend. Massage gently into the skin to firm it up and to combat stretch marks.

foot bath

Fresh leaves of bay, eucalyptus, lavender, lemon balm, thyme, marjoram, spearmint

Sprinkle handfuls of herbs into a large bowl. Add 2 teaspoons of salt and enough hot water to cover the feet and ankles. Soak feet for at least 10 minutes while breathing in the delicious aroma.

antiseptic wash

Among oils with antiseptic action are thyme, lavender, tea tree, and eucalyptus. Add 8 drops of one of these to a small bowl of water and apply to minor wounds.

Essential oils should not be used undiluted, nor taken internally except on medical advice.

Essential herbal oils or
fresh herbs steeped in
hot water can be used
to create a wide variety
of bathroom tonics—or
simply to enhance the
luxury of bathing.

cooking with herbs

vinegars, dressings, oils, and butters

Vinegars and dressings take on a slightly exotic flavor when combined with herbs, and there are many herbs that are good for this purpose. Flavored vinegars enhance fruit syrups and salad dressings—or can be used to deglaze a pan in which meat or fish has been fried.

tarragon vinegar

2 sprigs of tarragon (or thyme, lavender, or chives)
2 cups (500 ml) white wine vinegar

Makes 2 cups (500 ml)

Put the herb in the vinegar and leave in a warm sunny place for 3 or 4 days to let the flavor develop. Use as required.

tarragon vinegar dressing

1 tablespoon tarragon vinegar
1/4 cup hazelnut oil
2 tablespoons extra virgin olive oil
1/2 teaspoon sugar
salt and freshly ground black pepper

Make the tarragon vinegar as described above. Then stir all the ingredients and use as required.

mixed herb dressing

The different combinations of herbs that can be used to make this dressing are virtually endless.

2 tablespoons chopped mixed herbs: basil, chervil, chives, parsley, and mint
1/2 cup (125 ml) extra virgin olive oil
1 tablespoon balsamic vinegar
1 tablespoon Dijon mustard
1 garlic clove, lightly crushed
salt and freshly ground black pepper

Makes 2/3 cup (150 ml)

Beat the chopped herbs into the olive oil. Beat in the vinegar and mustard. Season to taste, then add the garlic. Use at once or store in the refrigerator for up to 2 days. Return the dressing to room temperature before use.

cilantro, soy, and sesame dressing

In addition to giving a refreshing zing to hearty vegetable salads, this dressing is delicious trickled over broiled chicken or sautéed and sliced duck breast.

2 tablespoons chopped cilantro
1 tablespoon dark soy sauce
1 teaspoon clear honey
1 teaspoon wholegrain mustard
2 teaspoons rice vinegar
1 tablespoon sesame oil
1/3 cup peanut oil

Makes 1/2 cup (125 ml)

Beat all the ingredients together and use as required.

fragrant Thai oil

This subtly spiced oil is wonderful trickled over steamed fish or added to marinades.

2 stalks of lemongrass, halved lengthwise
6 kaffir lime leaves or lime zest
2 slices galangal or fresh ginger
1 tiny red chile
2¹/₂ cups (600 ml) sunflower oil

Makes about 2¹/₂ cups (600 ml)

Lightly crush the herbs and aromatics and put them in a wide-necked bottle. Top up with the sunflower oil. Leave the oil to infuse for 7–10 days in a cool place before using.

rosemary, garlic, and pepper oil

To savor the delights of this pungently aromatic oil, use it as a dip for focaccia or ciabatta bread. An alternative is to trickle it over a freshly baked pizza (see page 98).

4 sprigs of rosemary
2 garlic cloves, sliced
1 tablespoon black peppercorns, lightly crushed
2¹/₂ cups (600 ml) extra virgin olive oil

Makes about 2¹/₂ cups (600 ml)

Put the rosemary, garlic, and peppercorns into a small saucepan with the olive oil. Heat gently until just boiling and simmer for 1 minute. Let cool, then infuse overnight. The next day, strain the infused oil into a clean bottle and add a sprig of rosemary and a few whole black peppercorns for decoration.

basil oil

You can enhance the flavor of a tomato salad and add color contrast by tossing the tomatoes gently in basil oil.

³/₄ cup (25 g) basil (or parsley) leaves
1¹/₄ cups (300 ml) extra virgin olive oil
a pinch of salt

Makes about 1 cup (250 ml)

Put the basil leaves, oil, and salt in a food processor and blend to a vivid green paste. Infuse overnight, then strain the oil through cheesecloth. Use the oil as required or store it in the refrigerator. Return it to room temperature before use.

thyme, lemon, and chile oil

For a quick supper, toss cooked pasta in a good dash of this oil, then top with sautéed mushrooms and a sprinkling of freshly grated pecorino cheese.

4 sprigs of thyme
4 pieces of lemon zest, cut into thin strips
2 small red chiles, finely sliced
2¹/₂ cups (600 ml) extra virgin olive oil

Makes about 2¹/₂ cups (600 ml)

Put the thyme, lemon strips, and sliced chiles in a bottle and add the oil. Infuse for 7–10 days, then strain into a clean bottle.

Combining herbs and oils is a terrific way both to preserve the herbs and to jazz up the oils. Flavored oils shouldn't be confined to salads. Use in marinades, trickle over broiled or grilled meat or fish—or pour into a dish and serve as a dip with a selection of freshly baked breads.

Herb butters add a lovely finishing touch to cooked fish or chicken and are easy to make. Simply beat your favorite herb into some softened butter, adding a little pepper or lemon juice. Pat into a roll, cover with plastic wrap, and chill until needed.

fennel and lemon butter

The flavor of fennel goes well with fish. For a very satisfying result, melt 1 tablespoon of the butter into a piece of fried salmon fillet.

1 stick (100 g) lightly salted butter, softened
2 tablespoons chopped fennel fronds
grated zest of half a lemon
a little freshly ground black pepper

Makes about 1/2 cup (100 g)

Put the butter, fennel, lemon zest, and pepper in a bowl and beat them until the butter is evenly speckled green.

cilantro and scallion butter

The pungency of cilantro and the sweetness of scallion are a wonderful combination with mashed potatoes.

1 stick (100 g) lightly salted butter, softened
2 tablespoons chopped cilantro
1 scallion, finely chopped

Makes about 1/2 cup (100 g)

Follow the method for making fennel and lemon butter, but replace the fronds of fennel with the cilantro and scallion.

pepper and chive butter

Fillets of roasted cod or other white fish taste even better when topped with this mildly onion-flavored butter.

1 stick (100 g) lightly salted butter, softened
2 tablespoons chopped chives
1 tablespoon mixed peppercorns, lightly crushed

Makes about 1/2 cup (100 g)

Follow the method for making fennel and lemon butter, but replace the fronds of fennel with the chives and peppercorns.

snacks and appetizers

ricotta baked with fresh herbs and chile

This is an easy way to cook ricotta that makes an ideal light lunch. Small rounds of ricotta are available from most Italian gourmet stores—or use wedges cut from a larger cheese.

1 lb. (500 g) ricotta cheese
2 garlic cloves, sliced
1 red chile, seeded and sliced
1/2 teaspoon lightly crushed coriander seeds
1/4 cup extra virgin olive oil
4 fresh bay leaves, lightly crushed
1 tablespoon freshly grated Parmesan cheese,
    plus extra to serve
salt and freshly ground black pepper
basil oil (page 90) or salsa verde (page 96)
    and toasted bread, to serve

Serves 4–6

Put the ricotta in a foil-lined baking dish. Put the garlic, chile, coriander seeds, and oil in a bowl and stir. Drizzle the oil mixture over the cheese and tuck the bay leaves underneath.

Sprinkle Parmesan, salt and pepper over the ricotta and bake in a preheated oven at 375°F (190°C) for 20 minutes, basting halfway through.

Serve the ricotta spread onto toasted bread sprinkled with basil oil or salsa verde. Serve topped with a little grated Parmesan.

Herb-based sauces or spreads can be served as dips for crudités or spooned onto broiled or grilled fish or poultry. Zhatar is a Middle Eastern street snack traditionally sold rolled up in a cone of paper with hard-cooked eggs.

salsa verde

¾ cup (25 g) parsley leaves
⅓ cup (15 g) mixed herbs, such as basil, chives, cilantro, and mint
1 garlic clove, chopped
6 green olives, pitted
1 tablespoon capers, rinsed and drained
2 anchovy fillets, rinsed and chopped
1 teaspoon Dijon mustard
2 teaspoons lemon juice
½ cup (125 ml) extra virgin olive oil
salt and freshly ground black pepper
vegetables and bread, to serve

Serves 6

Put all the ingredients, except the oil, in a food mixer and blend to a smooth paste. Gradually blend in the oil to form a sauce, then add salt and pepper to taste. Serve as a dip with fresh bread and raw or cooked vegetables.

zhatar

⅓ cup (15 g) thyme leaves
1½ tablespoons sesame seeds, toasted
¼ teaspoon salt

Serves 4

Put the ingredients in a mixer and work to a fine powder. Serve with hard-cooked eggs.

zhug

¾ cup (25 g) cilantro leaves
2–4 garlic cloves
1 teaspoon caraway seeds
1 teaspoon cumin seeds
seeds from 3 cardamom pods
1 large red chile, seeded and diced
2 tablespoons extra virgin olive oil
salt and freshly ground black pepper

Serves 4

Put all the ingredients in a food processor and blend until smooth. Add salt and pepper to taste and serve with grilled pita or lavash bread.

little pizzas with herb oil

This is a variation on hot garlic bread, in which small, thin pizza crusts are doused in rosemary, garlic, and pepper oil.

1 cup (150 g) white bread flour
1 teaspoon quick-rising active
  dry yeast
1 teaspoon salt
1 tablespoon extra virgin
  olive oil (or a flavored oil)

herb topping
2 large garlic cloves, sliced
leaves from 4 sprigs of rosemary
rosemary, garlic, and pepper
  oil (page 90)

Makes 4 small or 2 large pizzas

Sift the flour into the bowl of a food mixer and stir in the yeast and salt. With the dough hook turning, slowly pour in the oil and about ½ cup (125 ml) water heated to 120°F (48°C), to form a slightly sticky dough.

Knead for 10 minutes. Shape the dough into a ball. Put it in a greased bowl, cover with plastic wrap, and let rise for about 1 hour until the ball has doubled in size. Heat the oven to 450°F (230°C) and put a pizza stone or cookie sheet on the top shelf to heat.

Punch down the dough and divide it into 2 or 4 pieces. Put one piece on a floured surface and roll it out to form a thin, round crust. Mix the rosemary leaves and garlic with 6–8 tablespoons rosemary, garlic, and pepper oil and sprinkle a little of the mixture over the pizza crust.

Transfer the crust to the heated pizza stone or cookie sheet and bake for 10–12 minutes until puffed and golden. Sprinkle with a little extra rosemary, garlic, and pepper oil. Continue to roll out and cook the pizzas one at a time, eating them as they come out of the oven.

Vietnamese herb and shrimp rolls

Rice noodles, shrimp, and fragrant herbs are rolled up in rice paper wrappers and served with *nuóc cham*—a traditional Vietnamese dipping sauce.

Start by making the **nuóc cham**. Put the fish sauce, sugar, chile, and lime juice in a bowl. Add 2 tablespoons water and let infuse for 1 hour.

Cook the noodles in a large saucepan of lightly salted, boiling water for 3 minutes. Drain and refresh them in cold water. Drain again. Mix the noodles with 1 tablespoon of the dipping sauce.

To rehydrate the rice paper wrappers, dip them one by one into a bowl of cold water for a few seconds until soft. Lay each wrapper flat and top with a small handful of cooked noodles, 2 or 3 shrimp, a few pea shoots or bean sprouts, and a few herb leaves.

Fold over the ends of the wrappers and roll up to enclose the filling. Serve with the dipping sauce.

nuóc cham
3 tablespoons fish sauce
2 tablespoons sugar
1 large red chile, seeded and finely chopped
juice of ¹/₂ lime

1 bundle (2 oz./60 g) of beanthread or vermicelli rice noodles
12 small rice paper wrappers (available from Chinese supermarkets)
24–36 large cooked shrimp, shelled
1 cup (50 g) pea shoots or bean sprouts
12 Thai basil leaves (optional)
12 mint leaves
12 cilantro leaves

Serves 6

entrées

sea bass with fragrant Thai oil

For this dish you need either 2 woks or 2 large bamboo steamers. The easiest way to cook the fish is to lay them on large pieces of foil and put these on the racks of the woks or in the bottom of the steamers, so all the delicious juices settle in the foil.

Wash and dry the sea bass inside and out, and slash each side diagonally several times with a sharp knife. Put 2 fish on each of 2 large sheets of foil.

Mix the ginger, onion, and garlic in a bowl. Put some of the mixture into each cavity and add a few slices of lime and some cilantro sprigs. Sprinkle the rest over the fish.

Mix the tamari, mirin, and 2 tablespoons of the Thai oil together in a pitcher or bowl, then trickle the mixture over the fish. Put each foil package on racks set in 2 separate woks or into the bottom of 2 steamers. Cover tightly with lids and steam for 12 minutes. Remove from the heat, but leave undisturbed for 5 minutes longer.

Sprinkle each fish with chopped cilantro and serve it with the juices, steamed rice, and steamed Chinese greens.

4 sea bass, 1 lb. (500 g) each, drawn and scaled
2 inches (5 cm) fresh ginger, peeled and sliced
4 scallions, finely chopped
2 garlic cloves, sliced
1 lime, sliced
4 large sprigs of cilantro
1/4 cup tamari (Japanese soy sauce)
2 tablespoons mirin (sweetened Japanese rice wine)
1/3 cup fragrant Thai oil (see page 90)
chopped cilantro leaves, steamed rice, and Chinese greens, to serve

Serves 4

red mullet saltimbocca
with orange and sage

The Italian saltimbocca of veal scallop topped by prosciutto ham and sage inspired this dish. Red mullet is a rich fish, able to take the strong flavors of both ham and herb. The sweet/sharp sauce of orange and capers is a perfect foil.

2 oranges
8 large red mullet fillets, scaled
freshly ground black pepper
8 slices prosciutto
16 large sage leaves
3 tablespoons extra virgin olive oil
2 tablespoons (25 g) lightly salted butter
2 tablespoons capers, rinsed and drained
⅓ cup (75 ml) white wine

Serves 4

Peel and segment one of the oranges, reserving the juices in a bowl. Squeeze the juice of the other orange into the bowl.

Wash and dry the fish fillets and season with pepper. Lay the prosciutto slices flat and top each with a fillet and a sage leaf. Drizzle a little oil over the top. Starting from one narrow end, carefully roll up each piece of ham, enclosing the fillet, and secure it with a toothpick.

Heat the remaining oil and the butter together in a skillet with a heatproof handle. Add the rolls of fish and quickly brown them on all sides. Add the capers, wine, orange juice, and remaining sage leaves. Cover with a layer of foil and bake in a preheated oven at 400°F (200°C) for 8 minutes. Remove from the oven, transfer the rolls to a warm plate, and let rest for 5 minutes.

Meanwhile, add the orange segments to the skillet and heat through on top of the stove. Serve the saltimbocca with the sauce, a green salad, and some bread to mop up the delicious juices.

chile beef with avocado and cilantro salsa

The chile-marinated steaks can be broiled or
cooked on an outdoor grill. The heat of the chile
sauce is tempered by the coolness of the avocado
and the sour cream. For a great picnic sandwich,
let the steaks cool, then slice them and stuff each
into a pita pocket with a spoonful of the salsa
and another of sour cream.

4 beef filet mignons, about 8 oz. (250 g) each
2 tablespoons hot chile sauce or harissa paste
2 tablespoons olive oil
¼ cup (60 ml) sour cream
sprigs of cilantro, to serve

avocado and cilantro salsa
1 large ripe Hass avocado
2 ripe tomatoes, peeled, seeded, and diced
freshly squeezed juice of ½ to 1 lime
1 garlic clove, crushed
1 small red chile, seeded and diced
2 tablespoons chopped cilantro
1 tablespoon extra virgin olive oil
salt and freshly ground black pepper

Serves 4

Put the steaks in a shallow dish and rub them all
over with the chile sauce and oil. Marinate at room
temperature for 1–4 hours.

Just before cooking the steaks, cut the avocado in half
and remove the pit. Using a teaspoon, scoop the flesh
into a bowl. Stir in the tomato, lime juice, garlic, chile,
cilantro, and oil. Season with salt and pepper.

Heat a stove-top grill pan for 3–4 minutes until it is very
hot. Add the steaks and cook for 2 minutes each side.
Set aside to rest for 5 minutes.

Serve the steaks topped with the avocado and cilantro
salsa, the sour cream, and sprigs of cilantro.

1 chicken, about 3½ lb. (1.75 kg)
¾ cup (25 g) fresh curry leaves or
　⅓ cup (15 g) dried
1 stick (100 g) lightly salted butter
1 lemon, halved
1 whole head of garlic,
　cloves separated
salt and freshly ground black pepper

Serves 4

butter-roasted chicken with curry leaves

In some neighborhoods, the leaves of the curry plant are sold fresh or dried at Asian food stores. If they are not available, substitute sprigs of tarragon.

Wash the chicken and pat dry with paper towels. Season the cavity with salt and pepper and add a couple of sprigs of curry leaves. Cut several slashes in the flesh of each thigh. Finely chop (or tear) most of the remaining curry leaves. Put them in a bowl and beat in the butter with a wooden spoon.

Release the skin of the chicken from the flesh by inserting 4 of your fingers under the skin at the neck end. Lift the skin away from the breast meat and push half the butter mixture under it, smoothing until it is flat. Rub the remaining butter all over the outside of the skin, pushing it down into the slashes. Squeeze the juice of 1/2 lemon over the chicken and put the other half into the cavity.

Arrange the garlic cloves and remaining curry leaves in a roasting pan. Put the chicken on top and roast in a preheated oven at 400°F (200°C) for about 1 hour 5 minutes. Pierce the thickest part of the thigh with a skewer, penetrating as far as the joint: if the juices run clear, the chicken is cooked through. Let it rest for 5 minutes before carving.

spring herb risotto

The flavors of the herbs blend with the creaminess of the rice and cheese in this light, fragrant risotto. It is particularly good topped with a seared fillet of salmon or sautéed cod.

1 cup (50 g) shredded baby spinach leaves
1½ cups (50 g) chopped mixed herbs, such as
    chervil, chives, mint, parsley, and tarragon
¼ cup extra virgin olive oil
1 onion, finely chopped
2 garlic cloves, crushed
2 small leeks, well washed, trimmed, and sliced
1½ cups (300 g) arborio rice
⅔ cup (150 ml) dry white wine
¼ cup Mascarpone cheese
½ cup (50 g) freshly grated Parmesan cheese, plus
    extra to serve
salt and freshly ground black pepper

Serves 4

Put 5 cups (1.25 liters) water in a saucepan and heat to a rolling boil. Add the spinach and herbs, return to a boil, and immediately strain, reserving the liquid. Refresh the spinach and herbs under cold water. Pat dry with paper towels and set aside.

Heat the oil in a deep fryer. Add the onion, garlic, and leek and fry slowly for 10 minutes. Add the rice and stir the mixture over the heat for 1 minute until all the grains are glossy. Pour in the wine and boil until almost totally evaporated.

In a separate saucepan, heat the reserved herb water until just simmering. Add the water to the rice, 1 ladle at a time, and simmer, stirring, until absorbed, before adding more. Repeat until all the water has been used and the rice is tender but firm.

Stir in the spinach, herbs, and Mascarpone and Parmesan cheeses. Cover and let stand for 5 minutes. Season with salt and pepper. Serve with extra Parmesan.

accompaniments

mixed leaf and herb salad with pine nut dressing

The pine nuts add a rich, creamy flavor and texture to this salad dressing, which perfectly complements the aromatic herbs and leaves. Mix a good selection of fresh herbs—basil, chervil, chives, dill, mint, and parsley, for example—with salad leaves such as arugula, romaine, frisée, ruby chard, dandelion greens, and mizuna.

6 cups (500 g) mixed leaves and 2½ cups (100 g)
mixed herbs

pine nut dressing
2 tablespoons pine nuts
¼ cup extra virgin olive oil
2 teaspoons sherry vinegar
salt and freshly ground pepper

Serves 4

Put the salad leaves and herbs in a very large bowl.

To make the dressing, heat 2 tablespoons of the oil in a skillet. Add the pine nuts and sauté for 3–4 minutes until evenly golden. Let cool.

Using a mortar and pestle, smash the nuts until they are mushy. Stir in the remaining oil. Add the vinegar, and season to taste. Pour the dressing over the salad and toss well until all the leaves are coated. Serve at once.

charred leek salad with tarragon vinegar dressing

In this "smoky" salad the charred peppers and leeks are well set off by the sharpness of the tarragon-infused vinegar dressing, which must be made in advance.

2 small red bell peppers
12 oz. (350 g) baby leeks, well washed
*   and trimmed*
olive oil
1 cup (125 g) French beans, trimmed
3 cups (125 g) baby spinach leaves
½ cup (50 g) pitted black olives
1 quantity tarragon vinegar dressing (see page 89)
salt and freshly ground pepper
Parmesan shavings, to serve

Serves 4

Heat a large stove-top grill pan for 3 minutes. Add the whole peppers and cook for 10–15 minutes, turning occasionally, until charred all over. Transfer to a bowl, cover with a clean dry cloth, and let cool.

Toss the leeks in a little oil. Add to the grill pan and cook over low heat for 10–12 minutes until evenly charred. Let cool and cut in half crosswise. At the same time, blanch the beans in a large saucepan of lightly salted, boiling water for 3–4 minutes. Drain, refresh under cold water, and pat dry.

Slip the skins off the peppers, cut them in half, and remove all of the seeds. Cut the flesh into strips and toss the strips with the charred leeks and the beans. Arrange on a large plate. Add the spinach leaves and olives to the salad. Sprinkle with plenty of the salad dressing. Add the Parmesan shavings and serve at once.

smashed celery root with horseradish

The grated horseradish makes this deliciously rich "smash" a good partner for roast beef—or substitute chopped mint for the parsley and serve with broiled lamb chops.

¼ cup extra virgin olive oil, plus extra to mash
2 garlic cloves, crushed
6 scallions, trimmed and chopped
3¼ cups (500 g) peeled and finely diced
  celery root
3¼ cups (500 g) peeled and finely diced potatoes
2 inch piece of horseradish, peeled and finely
  grated (or 3 tablespoons ready-grated)
1¼ cups (300 ml) vegetable stock
2 tablespoons chopped flat-leaved parsley
salt and freshly ground black pepper

Serves 4

Heat the oil in a saucepan. Add the garlic and onion and sauté slowly for 5 minutes. Remove with a draining spoon and set aside. Add the celery root, potatoes, and horseradish to the pan and sauté for 5 minutes.

Pour the stock into the saucepan and bring to a boil. Cover and simmer for 25–30 minutes until the vegetables are tender. Remove the lid and boil until the liquid is reduced to the point where almost nothing remains and the mixture is sticky.

Stir in the reserved garlic and onion. Add the parsley, salt, and pepper and mash coarsely with a fork, beating in more olive oil to taste.

slow-roasted tomato salad with opal basil

This pretty salad can be served either as an accompaniment, a light lunch, or an appetizer. When opal basil leaves are not available, ordinary green basil can be used instead.

6 ripe tomatoes, halved
1 tablespoon olive oil
12 oz. mozzarella cheese (preferably buffalo
  mozzarella)
a few sprigs opal basil
1 quantity basil oil (see page 90)
balsamic vinegar
baby salad leaves such as mizuna
salt and freshly ground black pepper

Serves 4

Put the halved tomatoes in a small roasting pan in a single layer. Sprinkle with the olive oil and season liberally with salt and pepper. Roast in a heated oven at 300°F (150°C) for 3 hours until shrunken and glossy. Let cool.

Just before serving, tear the mozzarella into small pieces and arrange on a large plate. Add the tomato halves, then sprinkle the opal basil leaves over the tomatoes and cheese. Trickle a generous amount of the basil oil and a little vinegar over the salad. Season to taste with salt and pepper, and serve the salad topped with salad leaves.

sweet things

apricots poached in tarragon syrup

A delicately flavored tarragon and vanilla syrup perfumes the fresh apricots while they cook and then cool.

⅔ cup (125 g) sugar
2 pieces lemon zest, cut into thin strips
1 vanilla bean, split lengthwise
6 large sprigs of tarragon, lightly crushed
12 apricots, halved and pitted
1 tablespoon tarragon vinegar (see page 89)
*   or lemon juice*
vanilla ice cream or thick, plain yogurt, to serve

Serves 6

Put the sugar and 1¼ cups (300 ml) water in a wide saucepan and heat slowly to dissolve the sugar. Add the strips of lemon zest, the vanilla bean, and the tarragon sprigs. Bring to a boil.

Add the apricots and simmer slowly for about 5 minutes until soft. Remove the pan from the heat. Stir in the tarragon vinegar or lemon juice and let cool.

Serve with ice cream or yogurt.

strawberry, melon, and basil salad

This fragrant concoction is best served slightly chilled. The pairing of strawberries and basil is surprisingly good, but other herbs such as mint, lemon verbena, and lemon balm work equally well.

1 cantaloupe melon, halved, seeded, sliced, and peeled
1 basket (250 g) strawberries, hulled and halved
¾ cup (180 ml) Muscat de Beaumes de Venise or other sweet wine
a few basil leaves

Serves 4

Put the slices of melon in a large bowl with the strawberries. Pour the wine over the fruit and chill for 30 minutes. Top with the basil leaves and serve.

lemon and rosemary posset with raspberries

The posset in this recipe is a chilled creamy pudding, although originally, in the Middle Ages, a posset was a hot drink. Rosemary goes well with lemon and is excellent in creamy puddings, such as this. Prepare the posset in advance and chill it overnight in individual dishes.

1½ cups (600 ml) double cream
4 large sprigs of rosemary, washed and bruised
½ cup (100 g) sugar
½ cup freshly squeezed lemon juice
1 cup (125 g) raspberries
1 tablespoon framboise liqueur or crème de cassis

Serves 6

Put the cream and rosemary sprigs in a saucepan and heat slowly to boiling point. Remove from the heat and leave to infuse for 20 minutes. Discard the rosemary.

Add the sugar to the cream and return to a boil. Simmer for 3 minutes. Stir in the lemon juice, then immediately pour the mixture into 6 small dishes. Chill overnight.

Marinate the raspberries in framboise or crème de cassis for 30 minutes. Spoon the fruit onto the possets and serve.

mint chocolate chip ice cream

Heating mint with milk and cream gives this ice cream a wonderfully fresh flavor.

2 cups (500 ml) whole milk
1¼ cups (300 ml) heavy cream
4 large sprigs of mint
5 egg yolks
½ cup plus 2 tablespoons (125 g) superfine sugar
3 squares (75 g) semisweet chocolate, cut into small dice

Serves 8

Put the milk, cream, and mint sprigs in a saucepan and heat slowly to boiling point. Remove from the heat and leave to infuse for 20 minutes. Return to boiling point.

Meanwhile, beat the egg yolks and sugar in a bowl. Stir in the hot milk mixture, and return it to the pan. Stir over low heat until the custard is thick enough to coat the back of a wooden spoon. Do not let the mixture boil or it will curdle. Strain into a clean bowl and leave until cold.

Freeze in an ice cream maker according to manufacturer's directions—or freeze in a plastic container, beating at hourly intervals until creamy and frozen.

Add the chocolate chips just before the mixture freezes. Serve immediately or freeze until required.

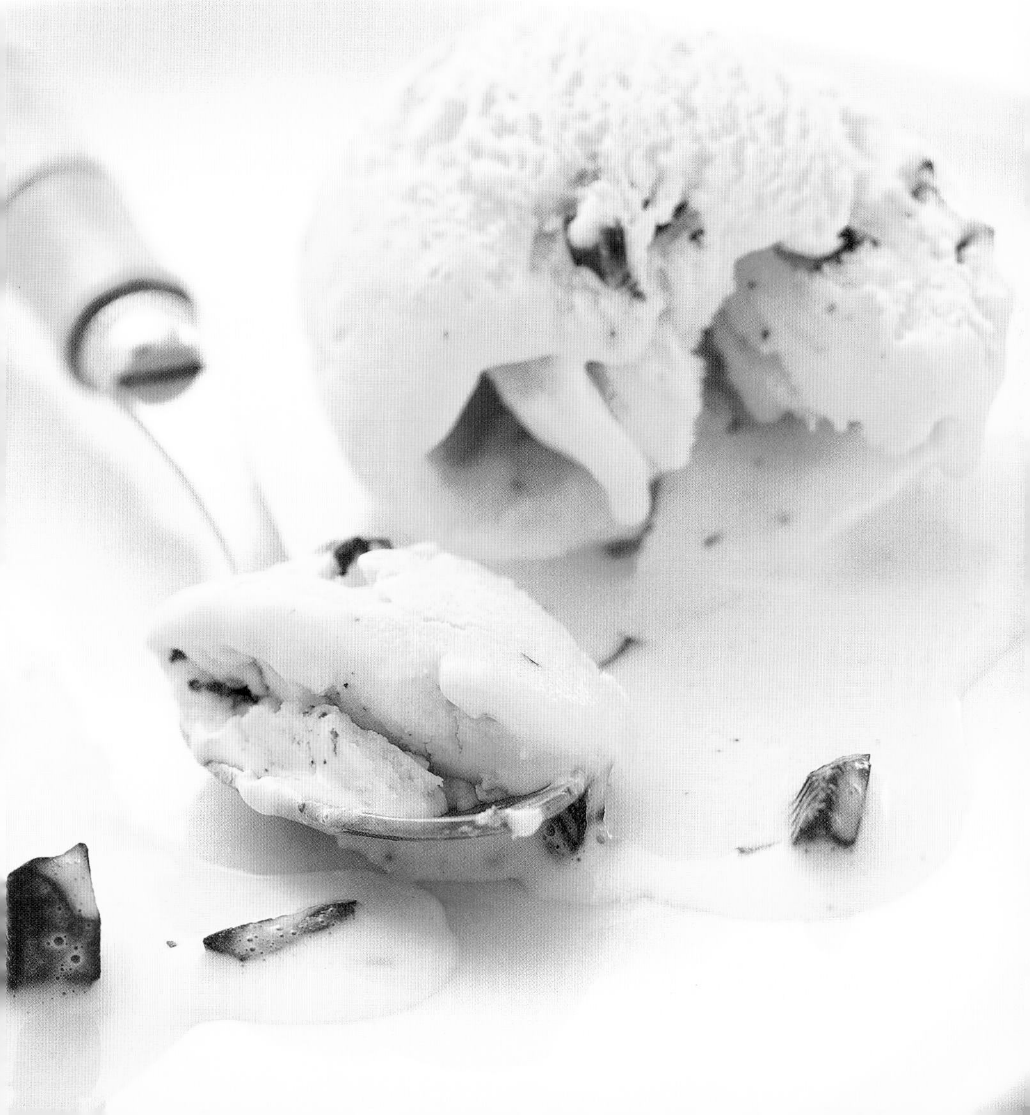

herbal coolers

Long Island tea with lemon verbena
4 tea bags (India tea is best)
a bunch lemon of verbena
2 limes, sliced
ice cubes
lemonade

Serves 4

Place the tea bags in a pitcher and add 4 cups (1 liter) cold water. Chill for 1 hour, then discard the tea bags.

Put the lemon verbena, slices of lime, and plenty of ice cubes in a large clean pitcher. Add the tea and top up with lemonade. Serve cold.

apple and lemongrass cordial
4 cups (1 liter) organic apple
*   juice (unsweetened)*
1 1/4 cups (250 g) sugar
4 large stalks of lemongrass,
*   halved lengthwise*
lemon wedges, ice cubes,
*   mineral water, and*
*   lemongrass stalks, to serve*

Makes about 3 cups (750 ml)

Put the apple juice and sugar in a saucepan and heat until the sugar dissolves. Add the lemongrass and simmer for 10 minutes. Let cool, then strain into a clean bottle.

To dilute, pour a little syrup into tall glasses. Add ice cubes and lemon, and top up with still or sparkling mineral water. Add a stalk of lemongrass to each glass and stir well.

melon and mint frappé

2 large ripe melons
1/2 cup (15 g) mint leaves
freshly squeezed juice of 2 limes
a little honey (optional)
ice cubes, to serve

Serves 4

Halve, seed, slice, and peel the melon and put the flesh in a blender. Add the mint leaves, lime juice, and honey if using it, and blend until smooth. Serve with ice cubes.

A–Z of herbs

A selection of herbs that flavor food or provide garden ornament.

(Heights given are the maximum heights to which plants can grow in optimum conditions. An asterisk against the zones of hardiness information indicates that zones vary according to species.)

Agastache foeniculum
Anise hyssop
Aromatic, hardy, but short-lived perennial that reaches a height of 2 ft (60 cm) when in flower. Heart-shaped leaves with scalloped edges. Purple or whitish flower spikes in summer. Sow seed in pots in heated propagator in spring. Grows in full sun in average soil, but does best in moist loam. Dried flower spikes and leaves can be added to potpourri.
Z: 6–9

Allium fistulosum
Welsh onion, scallion, spring onion
Hardy evergreen perennial that flowers from second year and reaches 2–3 ft (60–90 cm). Overwinters in coldest conditions. Sow in fertile soil in sun in spring, or divide clumps. Harvest whole onions, or chop leaves as you would chives.
Z: 4–9

Allium sativum
Garlic
Hardy perennial grown as an annual. Reaches 16–24 in (40–60 cm). Narrow leaves similar to those of leeks. Plant in fall in full sun; harvest as soon as leaves die down. Bulbs are delicious roasted; also used in marinades and salad dressings and to flavor meat. Wild garlic

(A. ursinum) needs moist woodland conditions; add leaves to salads and soups.
Z: 4–9

Allium schoenoprasum
Chives
Hardy perennial with fine green foliage and mauve or white pompom flowers. Depending on species or variety, grows to 12–16 in (30–40 cm) with a spread of 4–8 in (10–20 cm). Grow in moisture-retentive soil in full sun; divide crowded clumps in spring or fall. Flowers and leaves are used in salads, egg dishes, and soups. To prevent loss of flavor, add to hot dishes at the last moment.
Z: 3–9

Allium tuberosum
Chinese chives, garlic chives
Hardy perennial that grows to 16 in (40 cm). Leaves are as long as ordinary chives, but flattened, and have a strong aroma of garlic. Sow seed outside in late spring; divide clumps in spring. Good in salads and cooked dishes.
Z: 3–9

Aloe barbadensis
Aloe vera
Tropical. Succulent half-hardy perennial with fleshy spike-edged leaves. Can grow to a height of 2 ft (60 cm) in a large pot, but

is usually much smaller. Sow seed in pots in propagator at 70°F (21°C); germination is erratic—do not lose hope if nothing happens in the first year. Propagate from offshoots in summer. Use loam-based potting soil with added sand. Water sparingly and repot in spring. Plants can be grown outside in summer but must be overwintered in a frost-free place, at a minimum of 40°F (5°C). The gel from the aloe vera leaf soothes minor burns and cuts; it is also used in cosmetic preparations.

Aloysia triphylla syn. Lippia citriodora
Lemon verbena
Half-hardy deciduous perennial that grows to 10 ft (3 m) with a spread of 8 ft (2.5 m). Pale-green and lemon-scented lance-shaped leaves; terminal panicles of lilac-tinged white flowers. Likes full sun and free-draining light soil. If grown outside against a sunny wall, lemon verbena needs frost protection. A good deep mulch will keep the plant safe in milder climates; in colder areas, pot it up and overwinter in frost-free greenhouse. Grow from seed or softwood cuttings in spring. Take cuttings from ripened wood in late

summer. A relaxing tisane can be made from the leaves; also used to scent vinegars; dried lemon verbena is added to potpourri or herb pillows.
Z: 9

Anethum graveolens
Dill
Annual varying in height from 2 ft (60cm) to 5ft (150cm). Some varieties are suited to leaf or seed production. Dill needs well-drained, sandy soil and full sun. Sow seed in rows as soon as soil warms up in spring. Thin to about 8 in (20 cm) apart to make sturdy plants. Water in the morning; plants will run to seed if kept too dry. Sow in succession for a good kitchen supply. Excellent in fish dishes of all kinds.

Angelica archangelica
Angelica
Biennial or short-lived perennial that dies after flowering. Grows up to a height of 8 ft (2.5 m), but usually to 3–5 ft (1–1.5 m). A good ornamental plant in an herb bed in part-shade. Self-seeds copiously. Cooking angelica with rhubarb reduces the need for added sugar; stems can be candied. Should be used medicinally only on medical advice and never by diabetes sufferers.
Z: 4–9

Cichorium intybus
Chicory

Coriandrum sativum
Coriander

Helichrysum italicum
Curry plant

Anthriscus cerefolium
Chervil
Hardy annual that reaches
1–2 ft (30–60 cm) in
flower. Sow seed in light
soil. Part shade is best for
production of abundant
leaves. In a hot dry climate
it goes to seed prematurely.
Part of the traditional *fines
herbes* bundle.
Z: 3–8

Armoracia rusticana
Horseradish
Hardy perennial that grows
to 1–2 ft (60–90 cm).
'Variegata' has prettily
marked leaves in cream
and green and makes a
fine centerpiece in a herb
garden (though the flavor
is not as good or strong for
culinary use as that of the
non-variegated type).
Z: 3–10

Artemisia dracunculus
Tarragon
French tarragon grows
to 3 ft (90 cm); Russian
tarragon, *A. dracunculoides*,
is slightly taller, reaching
4 ft (1.2 m). Both have a
spread of 18 in (45 cm).
Grow in a dry sunny site
with winter protection.
Propagate French tarragon
from root cuttings; it is not
as hardy as the Russian
variety and has no viable
seed. Tarragon is good
with chicken and fish;
French tarragon has
much the better flavor.
Z: 4–7

Atriplex hortensis
Orach
Annual grown as a culinary
and an ornamental herb
that reaches 4 ft (1.5 m) or
more, with a spread of
12 in (30 cm); can grow
taller, depending on quality
of soil. Seed heads used in
cut-flower arrangements
in some countries. Use

tender young leaves in
cooking: a popular spinach
substitute in Europe.

Barbarea verna
Upland cress
Hardy biennial that grows
to 8–28 in (20–70 cm) with
a spread of 8 in (20 cm).
Sow in rich moist soil, in
summer for winter use and
in spring for summer use.
Prefers sun, but will grow
in all but deepest shade.
Peppery flavor of leaves
makes them a good
watercress substitute; use
before plants flower.
Z: 4–8

Borago officinalis
Borage
Hardy annual that grows to
24 in (60 cm); sometimes
plants overwinter and
grow into a second season.
Bristly branches, and leaves
with a strong cucumberlike
smell; blue or white starlike
flowers. Sow seed in
spring. Grow in light soil in
a sunny position. Edible
flowers can added to fruit
cups or crystallized for
decorative use. Borage may
cause contact dermatitis.

Buxus sempervirens
Boxwood
Hardy to half-hardy
evergreen used extensively
as an edging plant in herb
gardens. Grows from 3 ft
(1 m) to 15 ft (5 m), and
taller in old, unclipped
specimens. Leaves are
neatly egg-shaped to
elliptical, often glossy dark
to mid-green, and some
cultivars are variegated.
Boxwood grows in sun or
shade; prefers alkaline soil,
but as long as the ground
is not waterlogged, is
not too fussy. If a hedge
is planted, prepare the
soil well with compost
and well-rotted manure.

Take cuttings in spring or
summer. Boxwood has no
culinary use; all parts are
poisonous.
Z: 5–8

Calendula officinalis
Calendula
Hardy annual, but some
plants will overwinter
successfully. Grows to 24 in
(60 cm). Daisylike flowers,
single or double, vary in
color from pale cream to
deep orange. Whole plant
is aromatic. Calendula
grows in most soils in full
sun. Sow seed in spring or
fall. Self-sown seedlings are
capable of overwintering in
sheltered outside positions,
but do not rely on this.
Deadhead plants regularly
to extend flowering season.
Culinary and medicinal
plant; also used in cosmetic
preparations.

Chamaemelum nobile
Chamomile
Height varies from 2.5 in
(6 cm) to 24 in (60 cm)
depending on species or
cultivar. Non-flowering
'Treneague'—the type used
for chamomile lawns—is
increased by division and
the taking of cuttings,
as is the double-flowered
chamomile. For others, sow
seed in pots or straight into
the ground; use bottom
heat for pots in spring and
sow in ground when it has
warmed up. Grow in free-
draining soil in full sun.
Main uses are cosmetic
and medicinal.
Z: 4–8

Chenopodium bonus-
henricus
Good King Henry
Hardy perennial that can
reach 24 in (60 cm) with
a spread of 18 in (45 cm).
Sow seed in fertile soil in
spring in a sunny position.

Thin out to 10 in (25 cm) apart. Leaves used as a spinach substitute. Seeds are mildly laxative; do not use if you have kidney problems or rheumatism.
Z: 3–10

Cichorium intybus
Chicory
Hardy perennial reaching a height in flower of 3 ft (1 m). Leaves are long, blunt, and spear-shaped, with coarsely toothed edges. Blue flowers from summer to fall. Sow seed in spring in open sunny situation; prefers alkaline soil but will grow almost anywhere. Leaves are added to salads.
Z: 3–10

Coriandrum sativum
Cilantro, coriander
Tender annual growing to 24–28 in (60–70 cm) with a spread of 12 in (30 cm). 'Cilantro' is best for leaf production and 'Morocco' for seed. Sow seed in spring in a light well-drained soil when threat of frost has passed and soil has warmed up. Thin seedlings as they grow and keep watered for leaf production, but do not overwater. Seeds and leaves are used in cooking.

Cryptotaenia japonica
Mitsuba, Japanese parsley
Hardy perennial that grows to 12 in (30 cm) before flowering and 2–3 ft (60–90 cm) in flower. Leaf is like celery; small umbels of white flowers. Likes moist conditions in part shade. Grows in sun or in the shade of larger plants in moisture-retentive soil. Leaves and stems are used in cooking.
Z: 4–9

Curcuma longa
Turmeric
Perennial tropical herb of the ginger family. Can be grown as a pot plant in temperate climates, but needs winter protection. Grow in a peat and loam mix, with added grit or sharp sand. Likes warm moist air conditions. Don't overwater. Root is dried and ground into powder for culinary uses.

Cymbopogon citratus
Lemongrass
Perennial tropical grass with a strong lemon scent that reaches 2–3 ft (60–90 cm) in a greenhouse. Grow in pots from offshoots or seed. Use peat and loam mix, with added grit or sharp sand for good drainage. Do not overwater. Likes consistent warmth; reduce watering or do not water at all if it is overcast or raining for a long period. Used in Asian cooking.

Dianthus species
Pinks
Height varies from 8 in (15 cm) to 24 in (60 cm), depending on species. Grow from softwood cuttings in spring or heel cuttings in late summer. Some older cultivars have to be propagated directly after flowering; they may also be divided then. Grow in full sun in well-drained poor soil; most pinks also make good rock-garden plants. Dried petals are included in scented sachets.
Z: 5–8

Echinacea purpurea
Echinacea, purple coneflower
Hardy perennial that grows to 4 ft (1.2 m). Sow seed in early spring in a plug tray in greenhouse or propagator, or divide existing plants (in fall or spring) and plant in bed or herb garden. Grow in well-drained soil that will retain a bit of moisture in full sun. Echinacea seems to boost the immune system, helping the body to fight infection, and is used in the pharmaceutical industry. There are several good ornamental cultivars.
Z: 3–10

Eruca versicaria
Arugula
Half-hardy annual with a height of 2–3 ft (60–90 cm) in flower. Leaves are oval or lance-shaped; flowers are whitish with darker veining. Sow seed from spring on in partial shade in moisture-retentive soil. Sow in fall for winter salads. Cover with a cloche in severe weather. Hard frost and snow will kill arugula, but in mild areas it can be harvested for most of the winter. Adds peppery vigor to salads and cold dishes.

Eucalyptus citriodora
Eucalyptus
Tender evergreen tree. Can grow to more than 100 ft (30 m) in its native habitat. A good scented conservatory plant that can be taken outside to a sheltered patio. Sow seed in winter or spring. If kept in containers, feed during growing season. Used in cosmetics and pharmaceuticals.
Z: 9–10

Foeniculum vulgare
Fennel
Growing to 7 ft (2.1 m) in height, with a spread of 18 in (45 cm), this short-lived perennial is best sown straight into a permanent site. Cultivated for its culinary and medicinal purposes, fennel, especially the bronze form, is also a useful ornamental; its yellow flowers are carried in umbels in summer.
Z: 4–10

Fragaria vesca
Wild strawberry
Hardy perennial that grows to a height of 6–12 in (15–30 cm). Leaves are divided into heavily serrated leaflets. White-petaled flowers and sweet, scented fruit that may be red or white. Sow seed in late winter or early spring in pots in the greenhouse, or divide existing plants after fruiting. Grow in fertile moist soil in full sun or part shade.
Z: 5–9

Galium odoratum
syn. **Asperula odorata**
Sweet woodruff
Hardy perennial. Grows to 8 in (20 cm) in flower and has an indefinite spread. Whole plant is aromatic. Leaves are mid-green in whorls. Star-shaped white blooms appear in late spring or early summer. A plant for deep shade. Sow seed or propagate from root cuttings at almost any time, but the best time is after flowering; cut back and take small pieces of root to plant in pots or cuttings bed in part shade; water after planting. It will soon reshoot. Grows best in alkaline soil under deciduous shrubs and trees. Woodruff jelly is a delicacy in some parts of Europe.
Z: 3–9

Helichrysum italicum
Curry plant
Hardy evergreen perennial that grows to 24 in (60 cm) with a spread of up to 3 ft (1 m). Leaves are narrow

and silver-felted; yellow button flowers appear in summer. The whole plant has a strong curry scent. Not much used in the kitchen, rather as an ornamental in gardens. Increase by cuttings in spring or fall. Plant in well-drained soil in full sun. Prolonged wet combined with cold can kill the plant, so, in parts of the country where winters are cold and wet, grow in a large container or overwinter in a cold greenhouse.
Z: 8–9

Humulus lupulus
Hops

Hardy perennial herbaceous climber. Grows to 20 ft (6 m). Has male and female flowers on separate plants. Young leaves are heart-shaped; older leaves have three to five lobes. Whole plant is covered with tiny hooks. Sow in fall in pots and overwinter in a cold frame. Take cuttings or divide female plants in spring or early summer. The golden form of hop is a showy ornamental and can be used in the same way as green hops.
Z: 3–8

Hyssopus officinalis
Hyssop

Hardy semi-evergreen perennial that grows to a height of 32 in (80 cm) when in flower. Leaves are narrow and aromatic; flowers are blue, pink, or white, depending on variety. Rock hyssop, H.o. ssp. aristatus, is a good rock-garden or potted plant with dark-blue flowers. Grow in well-drained average soil in full sun. In pots it may need a feed boost if grown in the same soil for several years. Sow

seed in plug trays in heated propagator in spring. Cuttings can be taken in late spring and early summer from non-flowering shoots. Seed can also be sown straight into the ground. Thin out if grown as a hedge. Culinary and medicinal plant; use medicinally only on expert advice.
Z: 3–9

Juniperus communis
Juniper

Slow-growing hardy evergreen shrub or tree that reaches 25 ft (4 m) in height. Needle-like narrow leaves with sharp-pointed tips. Whole plant is aromatic. Sow seed in fall in pots and overwinter in cold frame or cold greenhouse. Take cuttings in spring or fall. Do not use juniper berries during pregnancy or if you suffer from kidney problems.
Z: 2–8

Laurus nobilis
Bay

Tree or small shrub that grows to 26 ft (8 m), with a spread of 20 ft (3 m) or more. Buy as a well-grown ornamental and use surplus leaves for bouquet garni or to flavor oil or vinegar. Pick leaves straight from tree or keep a few dried in a covered jar.
Z: 8–10

Lavandula species
Lavender

Hardy or half-hardy evergreen perennials. Vary in height, according to species or cultivar, from 12 in (30 cm) to 36 in (90 cm). One of the most popular plants in the modern garden. All species like an open sunny position in fertile well-drained soil.

Seed can be sown in fall or spring into pots or trays; overwinter fall-sown seed in cold greenhouse. Seed, except that from L. stoechas, is variable. Cut back plants after flowering, and for a neat bush trim again in spring. Leaves are all very narrow; flower spikes are usually mauve/purple, pale blue or dark blue. Culinary and medicinal herb that is also used in distilled form in cosmetics.
Z: 5–10*

Levisticum officinale
Lovage

Hardy perennial. Grows to 6 ft (2 m) with a spread of up to 3 ft (1 m) or more. Grow in rich, moist, well-drained soil in full sun or part shade; sow seed in fall outside, or in spring in pots in a propagator. Use young leaves in soups and salads; the flavor is better before flowering. Do not take in pregnancy or if you have kidney problems.
Z: 5–8

Lonicera species
Honeysuckle

L. periclymenum is a deciduous perennial that grows up to 23 ft (7 m). Its fragrant flowers with a pink/red blush are followed by (poisonous) red berries. L. japonica is a semi-evergreen deciduous perennial with a height of up to 30 ft (10 m); pale cream flowers turn yellow with age and are followed by black berries (also poisonous). Sow seed in fall in pots to overwinter outside or in cold frame. Take cuttings in summer or layer at any time. Will grow in sun or part shade in most soils.
Z: 4–11*

Malva sylvestris
Mallow

Biennial or short-lived perennial that, depending on variety, can grow to 5 ft (1.5 m). Rounded leaves on basal rosette resemble those of Alchemilla mollis, and those that grow up the stem are finely cut or ivy-shaped. Mallows will tolerate most soils, but in overly moist may need staking. Fertile soil in sun or part shade will suit the plants best. Sow seed in sfall and overwinter in cold frame, or sow in spring in cool greenhouse. Seed can also be sown in the garden where the plants are to flower. Used in cooking.
Z: 4–9

Melissa officinalis
Lemon balm

Hardy perennial that grows to 32 in (80 cm). The golden form, M. o. 'All Gold,' may need some protection in winter, so mulch with foliage and keep this in place with a cloche. Keep 'All Gold' out of full sun or it will scorch. Golden and variegated forms are fine ornamentals; all are good bee plants. Increase by cuttings or division in fall or spring. Loses its lemon fragrance when cooked, so use fresh in the kitchen.
Z: 4–9

Mentha
Mint

Grows to various heights depending on species; some are prostrate. Mint has spreading root runners and can be very invasive. The leaves of different species have different aromatic qualities. Most mint grows best in part or full shade. They need to be restrained to prevent them

from taking over entire beds, so plant in a deep plastic or tin container and sink the container into the ground. Cut back mints in midsummer to rejuvenate plants. Culinary and medicinal herb. Mint oil may cause an allergic reaction and must not be used on babies.
Z: 4–11*

Monarda didyma
Bee balm, bergamot, oswego tea
Hardy perennial that, depending on species or cultivar, grows to between 30 in (75 cm) and 36 in (90 cm), with a spread of 18 in (45 cm). Leaves are elliptical, sometimes toothed, with pointed tips. Flowers are in whorls; colors include pale purple, red, white, soft pink, and purple. All cultivars have to be increased by division or cuttings. Seed from species should be sown in pots or trays. Grow in part shade in moist rich soil; in moisture-retentive soil it will grow in full sun. Mainly grown in perennial flowerbeds for its flowers, but also has culinary and medicinal uses.
Z: 4–10

Myrrhis odorata
Sweet cicely
Hardy perennial that grows to between 2 ft (60 cm) and 3 ft (90 cm) in flower. Leaves are fernlike; small white flowers in large umbels. Sow seed in pots and overwinter in a cold frame because seeds need stratifying. Take root cuttings in spring or fall, and divide plants in spring. For best results, grow in well-drained poor soil. Cut back flower heads before they set seed.
Z: 3–7

Myrtus communis
Myrtle
Half-hardy evergreen shrub that grows to 10 ft (3 m). All parts are aromatic. In areas with cold wet winters and prolonged frosts, grow in containers and overwinter in a greenhouse or conservatory. In milder areas, simply protect from too much winter rain. Grow in well-drained soil in full sun. If grown in containers, add sand and bark to loam-based soil. Take softwood cuttings in spring and semi-ripe cuttings in late summer.
Z: 9–10

Ocimum basilicum
Basil
Annual. In temperate northern areas basil is best pot-grown, reaching 18 in (45 cm) with a spread of up to 12 in (30 cm). In warmer regions it can grow to twice that size or more, in the ground. Sow seed in spring either in the ground after frost, or in containers in a warm greenhouse or under lights. Transplant as soon as the plant is large enough to handle. Take care not to overwater. Great in salads, especially tomato salads, in pesto sauce, and with pasta.

Oenothera biennis
Evening primrose
Hardy biennial that can reach 4 ft (1.2 m). Lance-shaped leaves make a rosette in the first year, and in the second year the flower spike rises with large yellow, evening-scented flowers. Sow seed in spring in pots, trays, or in the place where you want it to grow. Grow in well-drained soil in a sunny position. Self-sows abundantly. Mainly medicinal, but all

parts are edible and can be steamed and eaten.
Z: 5–8

Origanum vulgare
Oregano, marjoram
Several species and varieties; most are hardy in light soil and grow to a height and a spread of up to 24 in (60 cm). Species can be grown in spring in pots or in situ; soil should be free-draining and alkaline. Will not thrive in waterlogged soils. Best in full sun. Cultivars will not come true from seed and cuttings should be taken in late spring; plants can also be divided in spring. Widely used in cooking. An infusion in the bath aids relaxation and a few drops of essential oil on the pillow promotes sleep.
Z: 5–9

Papaver somniferum
Opium poppy
Hardy annual. Grows to 90 cm (36 in). Sow seed in fall for early flowers and seeds, or in spring for later flowering, straight into the ground in a sunny, fertile, well-drained soil. Thin if necessary. Seeds are used in baking and salads. Other parts are used in pharmaceuticals.

Pelargonium species
Scented pelargoniums
Tropical. Half-hardy plants that, depending on variety and species, grow to varying heights, from 12–40 in (30 cm–1 m). Some species can be grown from seed but it is easier to grow them from cuttings, and all cultivars must be grown from cuttings. Take cuttings in summer or fall as plants are being cut back before overwintering in a frost-free site. Grow in full

sun in well-drained soil if in the ground. Reduce watering in fall and keep it to a minimum in winter. Essential oils are used in aromatherapy. The scented leaves are sometimes used to flavor cakes and puddings, but should be removed before serving.

Perilla frutescens
Perilla
Tender annual that makes a good ornamental in the flowerbed. Taller purple form can reach 3 ft (90 cm). Leaves resemble a stinging nettle; can also be confused with the "ruffles" type of basil. Start off in greenhouse or under lights. Transplant, and plant out once frosts are over. Grow in light well-drained soil in full sun or light shade. In cold areas grow in pots. Can stand cold a little better than basil, but likes similar treatment.

Petroselinum crispum
Parsley
Hardy biennial that grows to 12 in (30 cm), and to 24 in (60 cm) in flower. Greenish-white flowers in second year. Various forms with heavily curled foliage; others with uncurled, flat leaves. All are good for salads and flavoring. In some countries, seeds are chewed to cure bad breath. Also has a medicinal use, but avoid in pregnancy.
Z: 6–9

Pimpinella anisum
Anise
Half-hardy annual. Grows to 18 in (45cm) with a spread of 10 in (25cm). Sow seed in light well-drained soil in a sunny spot when frosts are over. Do not transplant; thin to 8 in (20 cm) apart. Gather

seeds on stalks in late summer as they ripen, and dry in paper bags. Seeds used in fruit dishes and Middle Eastern recipes.

Portulaca oleracea
Purslane

Half-hardy annual growing to 6 in (15 cm) with a spread of 12 in (30 cm). Green or golden leaves. Sow in pots for early planting or in rows in full sun; thin out and use early in season. Mild-flavored leaves are good in salads* and complement stronger-flavored herbs and spices.

Primula vulgaris
Primrose

Spring-flowering perennial. Height and spread of 6 in (15 cm). Club-shaped leaves grow from basal rosette. Pale-yellow flowers with delicate honey scent grow singly from the rosette. Grows in moist soil in sun or shade and tolerates heavy soils. Start seed in pots in fall. Leave outside in cold frame or grow fresh seed straight after harvest; germination can be erratic. Plants can be divided in fall.
Z: 5–9

Rosa species
Rose

Old-fashioned roses such as the scented apothecary's rose, *R. gallica* 'Officinalis,' were traditionally used in herb gardens. 'Officinalis' has a lax sprawling growth. Scented petals are used in cosmetics, to flavor food, and in potpourri.
Z: 2–9

Rosmarinus officinalis
Rosemary

Numerous cultivars, some upright, others prostrate. Prostrate group reaches a height of 12 in (30 cm). The largest rosemary has a height and a spread of up to 6 ft (2 m). *R. officinalis* can be grown from seed, but cultivars need to be propagated from soft or semi-ripe cuttings in spring or late summer; they can also be layered. Needs well-drained soil and a sunny position. Grows well in containers. Used in the kitchen, medicinally, and in cosmetic preparations, but avoid in pregnancy. Essential oil must not be taken internally.
Z: 7–10*

Rumex acetosa and R. scutatus
Common sorrel and buckler leaf or French sorrel

Common sorrel is a hardy perennial growing to 2–4 ft (60–120 cm) with a spread of 1 ft (30 cm). Buckler leaf sorrel grows to 6–18 in (15–45 cm) with a spread of 5–24 in (12.5–60 cm). Sow seed in spring in propagator from February on, or in late spring outside. Can be divided in spring or fall. Sorrel is a good culinary plant; also used in medicine and, with alum as a mordant, makes a yellow or green dye. Contains oxalic acid, and is poisonous in large doses. Avoid if you have kidney disease, kidney stones, rheumatism, or gout.
Z: 4–8

Salvia officinalis
Sage

Height and spread vary, depending on species, up to 3 ft (90 cm) in height and 28 in (70 cm) spread. Purple, golden, and tricolored sages are good ornamentals as well as culinary and medicinal plants. Ideal container plant for a sunny patio. Not all sages are hardy. *S. elegans* (with pineapple-scented leaves) needs to be overwintered in frost-free conditions. Grow from cuttings in spring and summer, and replace plants every few years as they become very woody. Grow in a light free-draining soil in full sun. Dried leaves can be added to potpourri.
Z: 5–8

Sambucus nigra
Elder

Deciduous hardy perennial shrub or tree that grows to a height of 10–23 ft (3–7 m) with a spread of up to 12 ft (3.5 m). Good ornamental for beds or wild hedgerows. Fruit must be cooked if used in the kitchen. Flowers used to make fritters and elderflower champagne. Traditionally, berries have been made into a cordial for relieving the symptoms of colds and coughs.
Z: 5–9

Sanguisorba minor
Salad burnet

Hardy evergreen perennial. Grows to a height of 8–24 in (20–60 cm) with a spread of 12 in (30 cm). Sow seed in spring or fall; deadhead regularly. Culinary and medicinal herb that deserves wider use in the kitchen. Has a slight cucumber taste and goes well with fish, cheese, and salads, especially in winter, when other herbs may be scarce.
Z: 4–8

Saponaria officinalis
Soapwort

Hardy perennial growing to 3 ft (90 cm) or more. Tumbling lax plant with lance-shaped oval leaves and clusters of single flowers, but 'Rubra Plena' has double flowers that are at first pink and turn red with age. Can be invasive. Sow seed in fall, as soon as ripe, in a cold frame. Plants appear in spring. Germination is sometimes erratic. Rootstock can be divided in fall or early spring. Soapwort has been used medicinally, in cosmetics, and as an ingredient of soap.
Z: 2–8

Satureja hortensis
Summer savory, bean herb

Half-hardy annual that reaches a height of 12 in (30 cm) in flower with a spread of 8 in (20 cm). Grows bushier if growing tips are harvested often. Sow seed outside when frosts are over, or sow in pots and transplant when soil warms up. Whole plant is aromatic. Use leaves before white or mauve flowers appear. Dries well, and is sold dried. In parts of Europe summer savory is used in almost every dish that incorporates beans.

Satureja montana
Winter savory, mountain savory

Semi-evergreen hardy perennial that grows to 12 in (30 cm) with a spread of 12 in (30 cm) or more depending on conditions. Narrow, lance-shaped leaves; white flowers. Whole plant is aromatic. Likes full sun and well-drained poor soil. Good ornamental in the right soil; suitable in rock gardens. Take cuttings in spring, or sow seed under lights or in greenhouse in early spring. Seed needs light

to germinate. In areas of high rainfall and heavy soil, overwinter some plants in containes, where watering can be minimized. Used to flavor soups, game, and other meats.
Z: 5–8

Sesamum indicum
Sesame
Annual tropical herb that grows to a height of 2–3 ft (60–90 cm). Needs long hot summers to produce its nutty seeds. Collect seeds as they ripen before the capsules burst open. Sow after frost danger is past. In cool areas grow under cover. Start in pots with a heated propagation mat to extend growing season. Leaves and seeds are used in cooking.

Symphytum officinale
Comfrey
Hardy perennial growing to 3 ft (1 m). Lance-shaped bristly leaves; depending on species or cultivar, flowers can be cream, yellow, blue purple, pink, or red. Sow seed in spring in garden; germination is erratic. Root cuttings or divisions produce plants more quickly. Grow in full sun or part shade; does best in deep moist soil. Used in organic gardening as a green manure.
Z: 4–9

Tanacetum parthenium
Feverfew
Hardy short-lived perennial that varies in height from 2 ft (60 cm) to 4 ft (120 cm); sometimes smaller, especially golden feverfew, 'Aureum,' which reaches 18 in (45 cm) in flower. Grow in rich soil in full sun. Deadhead often. Sow seed in spring or early fall; overwinter plants from

fall, sowing in cold frame or heated greenhouse. Feverfew is used to relieve migraines but side effects can be unpleasant.
Z: 4–9

Taraxacum officinale
Dandelion
Hardy perennial. Height in flower about 10 in (25 cm). Long, deeply toothed leaves grow from basal rosette; flowers are deep yellow. Sow seed in spring in pots or straight into soil. Root cuttings can also be taken. Leaves are added to salads; before use, cover plants for a few weeks so they become blanched and less bitter.
Z: 3–10

Thymus species
Thyme
Numerous species, some upright, others creeping. Creeping thymes reach about 1 in (2.5 cm) with a spread of 8 in (20 cm) or more. Shrubby thymes reach 12 in (30 cm) with a spread of 8 in (20 cm). Creeping thymes are useful as ground cover or for scented lawns in full sun. Seed of species can be sown on top of sandy soil. Cultivars are increased only by cuttings; creeping thymes can be increased by division. Deadhead after flowering. The plant is safely eaten in many dishes, but the oil should be used only on medical advice. Avoid in pregnancy.
Z: 4–9

Tropaeolum majus
Nasturtium
Half-hardy annual. Many cultivated forms that creep or are bushy, so height and spread can vary. Height is usually 8-12 in (20–30 cm), and spread can be 40 in

(1 m) or more. *T. m.* 'Alaska' has variegated leaves and yellow, orange or red flowers. Good plant for a sunny yard and well-drained poor soil. If it is too well fed, flower production will suffer. Sow early in pots, or in the growing site when danger of frost is past. Deadhead regularly. Use young flowers in salads. Seeds, flowers, and leaves are all edible, but treat with caution.

Urtica dioica
Nettle
Hardy perennial that grows to a height of 5 ft (1.5 m); the flowering tops can be even taller in good soil. Leaves are arrow-shaped and deeply serrated, with bristles that break off when touched. Grows in any soil in sun or shade. Roots can be divided and replanted. A good butterfly plant. Used medicinally, in cooking, in organic gardening, and as a dye plant.
Z: 3–10

Verbena officinalis
Vervain
Hardy perennial growing to 24–36 in (60–90 cm) when in flower. Leaves are deeply lobed; flowers pale lilac. Sow seed in spring in pots or straight into soil. Grows in any well-drained soil in full sun. Divide existing plants in spring or fall. Avoid in pregnancy.
Z: 4–8

Viola odorata
Violet
Hardy perennial that can reach a height of 8 in (20 cm), depending on species. Leaves, usually heart-shaped, grow from basal rosette. Scented flowers in a variety of colors; dog violet and wood

violet have blue or lilac flowers. Sow seed as soon as it ripens in fall and overwinter in a cold frame. Divide or take cuttings from cultivars or a good plant of a species in spring. Grows in moderately heavy fertile soil. Flowers can be used in herbal sachets and perfumes.
Z: 6–9

Viola tricolor
Johnny-jump-up, heartsease
Hardy perennial that is often grown as an annual. Reaches 12 in (30 cm). Scalloped mid-green leaves; tricolored "little face" flowers. Sow seed in spring in cold frame. Grows in most soils in sun or part shade. Culinary and medicinal herb.
Z: 4–9

Zingiber officinale
Ginger
Perennial tropical herb. Grown in a container from a division of its rhizome. Requires peat and loam mix with added sharp sand. Water freely in hot summer months; reduce watering toward winter. Widely used in eastern cuisines.
Z: 9–11

resources

**SUPPLIERS OF PLANTS
AND SEEDS**

Avant Gardens
710 High Hill Road
North Dartmouth
MA 02747-1363
(508)-998-8819
www.avant
gardensNE.com

The Banana Tree Inc.
715 Northampton Street
Easton, PA 18042
(610)-253-9589
www.banana-tree.com

Bluestone Perennials
7211 Middle Ridge Road
Madison
OH 44057-3096
(800)-852-5243
www.bluestone
perennial.com

Carroll Gardens
444 E. Main Street
Westminster
MD 21157
(800)-638-6334
www.carrollgardens.com

Catnip Acres Herb Farm
67 Christian Street
Oxford, CT 06478
(203)-888-5649
www.catnipacres.com

Companion Plants
7247 N. Collville
   Ridge Road
Athens, OH 45701
(740)-592-4643
www.companion
plants.com

The Cook's Garden
P.O. Box 535
Londonderry
VT 05148
(800)-547-9703
www.cooksgarden.com

DeBaggio Herbs
Catalog Dept.
43494 Conconully
   View Drive
Chantilly
VA 20152
(703)-327-6976
www.debaggioherbs.com

Filaree Farm
182 Conconully Highway
Okanogan
WA 98840
(509)-422 6940
www.filareefarm.com

Glasshouse Works
P.O. Box 97
Church Street
Stewart
OH 45778-0097
(800)-837-2142
www.rareplants.com

Goodwin Creek Gardens
P.O. Box 83
Williams
OR 97544
(800)-846-7359
www.goodwincreek
gardens.com

**Gurney's Seed
& Nursery Co.**
110 Capitol Street
Yankton
SD 57079
(800)-806-1972
www.gurneys.com

Harris Seeds
355 Paul Road
P.O. Box 24966
Rochester
NY 14624
(800)-514-4441
www.harrisseeds.com

Heronswood Nursery
7530 NE 288th Street
Kingston
WA 98346
(360)-297-4172
www.heronswood.com

Johnny's Selected Seeds
Foss Hill Road, RR 1
Box 2580
Albion
ME 04910
(207)-437-4301
www.johnnyseeds.com

Logee's Greenhouses
141 North Street
Danielson
CT 06239
(888)-330-8038
www.logees.com

Mellinger's Inc.
2310 W. South
   Range Road
North Lima
OH 44452
(800)-321-7444
www.mellingers.com

Nichols Garden Nursery
1190 Old Salem Road NE
Albany
OR 97321
(541)-928-9280
www.nicholsgarden
nursery.com

Park Seed
1 Parkton Avenue
Greenwood
SC 29647
(800)-845-3369
www.parkseed.com

**Peaceful Valley Farm
Supply**
P.O. Box 2209
Grass Valley
CA 95945
(888)-784-1722
www.groworganic.com

Piedmont Plant Company
807 N. Washington
   Street
P.O. Box 424
Albany
GA 31702
(800)-541-5185
www.plantfields.com

**Redwood City Seed
Company**
Box 361
Redwood City
CA 94064
(650) 325-7333
www.redwoodcity
seed.com

Sandy Mush Herb Nursery
316 Surrett Cove Road
Leicester
NC 28748
(828)-683-2014
www.brwm.org/
sandymushherbs

Seeds of Change
P.O. Box 15700
Santa Fe
NM 87506
(888)-762-7333
www.seedsofchange.com

Select Seeds
180 Stickney Hill Road
Union, CT 06076
(860)-684-9310
www.selectseeds.com

Shepherd's Garden Seeds
30 Irene Street
Torrington
CT 06790
(860)-482-0532
www.shepherdseeds.com

Stokes
P.O. Box 548
Buffalo
NY 14240
(800)-396-9238
www.stokeseeds.com

Territorial Seed Company
P.O. Box 158
Cottage Grove
OR 97424
(541)-942-9547
www.territorialseed.com

The Thyme Garden
20546 Alsea Highway
Alsea
OR 97324
(541)-487-8671
www.thymegarden.com

Tinmouth Channel Farm
P.O. Box 428 B
Tinmouth
VT 05773
(802)-446-2812

W. Atlee Burpee Seed Co.
300 Park Avenue
Warminster
PA 18974
(800)-888-1447
www.burpee.com

Wayside Gardens
1 Garden Lane
Hodges
SC 29695-0001
(800)-845-1124
www.waysidegardens.com

White Flower Farm
P.O. Box 50
Litchfield
CT 06759
(800)-503-9624
www.whiteflower
farm.com

CRAFT SUPPLIERS

Glenbrook Farms
Herbs & Such
15922 76th Street
Live Oak
FL 32060
(888)-716-7627
www.glenbrookfarm.com

Martha By Mail
P.O. Box 60060
Tampa
FL 33660-0060
(800)-950-7130
www.marthabymail.com

San Francisco Herb Co.
250 14th Street
San Francisco
CA 94103
(800)-227-4530
www.sfherb.com

Target Stores
33 South Sixth Street
Minneapolis
MN 55402
(888)-304-4000
www.target.com

NATIONAL ASSOCIATION

**The Herb Society
of America**
9019 Kirtland
  Chardon Road
Kirtland
Ohio 44094
(440)-256-0514
www.herbsociety.org

KEY TO HARDINESS ZONES

Except in the case of annual and tropical plants, hardiness zones are indicated in the A–Z of Herbs (pages 116–123). Note that these are guidelines, not absolutes. Extreme heat, cold, or wetness can affect a plant's survival in a given zone.

Zones are based on the average annual minimum temperature for each zone; the smaller number indicates the most northerly zone a plant can survive in; the higher number the most southerly zone the plant will tolerate.

Z1   below −50°F (−45°C)
Z2 −50° to −40°F (−45° to −40°C)
Z3 −40° to −30°F (−40° to −34°C)
Z4 −30° to −20°F (−34° to −29°C)
Z5 −20° to −10°F (−29° to −23°C)
Z6 −10° to 0°F (−23° to −18°C)
Z7   0° to 10°F (−18° to −12°C)
Z8   10° to 20°F (−12° to −7°C)
Z9   20° to 30°F (−7° to −1°C)
Z10 30° to 40°F (−1° to 4°C)
Z11 above 40°F (4°C)

index

picture credits and acknowledgments

Key: a = above, b = below, l = left, r = right, c = center

1 Linda Garman's home in London; 2l Bruisyard
Vineyard & Herb Centre, Bruisyard, Suffolk; 32–35, 36a,
37, & 39 Rosemary Titterington at Iden Croft Herbs,
Staplehurst, Kent; 40–41 Bruisyard Vineyard & Herb
Centre, Bruisyard, Suffolk; 41a Rosemary Titterington
at Iden Croft Herbs, Staplehurst, Kent; 41b photograph
© Jonathan Buckley; 42–43 Merryweather's Herbs in
Herstmonceux, East Sussex; 46 Rosemary Titterington at
Iden Croft Herbs, Staplehurst, Kent; 47 & 48 Bruisyard
Vineyard & Herb Centre, Bruisyard, Suffolk; 49
Rosemary Titterington at Iden Croft Herbs, Staplehurst,
Kent; 52–53 Bruisyard Vineyard & Herb Centre,
Bruisyard, Suffolk; 56–57 Linda Garman's home in
London; 58a Rosanna Dickinson's home in London; 58b
& 59 Mary MacCarthy's house in Norfolk; 60–61
Rosanna Dickinson's home in London; 64 & 65l Linda
Garman's home in London; 66–67 Linda Garman's
home in London; 68 Mary MacCarthy's house in
Norfolk; 70r & 76a Linda Garman's home in London;
76b, 77, & 80l Mary MacCarthy's house in Norfolk;
80r Linda Garman's home in London; 81 Mary
MacCarthy's house in Norfolk; 85 & 128 Rosanna
Dickinson's home in London.

Barbara Segall would like to thank Gisela Mirwis, for
her research, and Debbie Arden, who helped compile
the list of herb farms, nurseries, and seed suppliers.

Rose Hammick would like to thank Carol Hammick
and Adam Tindle for the use of the glasshouse and
vegetable garden, Claire Farrow and William Morris,
Zosia at White & Gray, Victoria Robinson, Amanda
and Sarah Vesey, Georgina Hammick, Katie Rudaz,
Richard Mole, Charlotte Packer, Clementine Young,
and Ashley Western.

The publishers would like to thank the following
organizations for providing information and
photographic locations:

Bruisyard Vineyard & Herb Centre
Church Road, Bruisyard
Saxmundham, Suffolk IP17 2EF, UK
+ 44-(0)1728-638281
*The 10 acre (4 hectare) site incorporates a vineyard, a
winery, a herb garden, a water garden, a children's play
area and a picnic area. Producers of award-winning
Bruisyard English wines and a wide selection of herbs.*
Pages 2l, 40–41, 47, 48, 52–53.

Iden Croft Herbs
Staplehurst, Kent TN12 0DH, UK
+ 44-(0)1580-891-432
www.herbs-uk.com
*Plants, seeds, and garden visits. Themed show
gardens include culinary, medicinal, patio, potpourri,
and cottage gardens.*
Pages 32–35, 36a, 37, 39, 41a, 46, 49.

Mary MacCarthy
+ 44-(0)1328-730-133
Decorative paintwork and murals.
Pages 58b, 59, 68, 76b, 77, 80l, 81.

Merryweather's Herbs
Merryweather's Farm, Chilsham Lane
Herstmonceux, East Sussex BN27 4QH, UK
+ 44-(0)1323-833-316
www.morethanjustagarden.co.uk
*Owners Ian & Liz O'Halloran. A unique project
creating 5$\frac{1}{2}$ acres (2.2 hectares) of gardens and
wildlife habitat and incorporating a small nursery.*
Pages 42–43.